Fully Persuaded Faith

By David Cooley

Fully Persuaded Faith

Bible References:
- King James Version (KJV)
- Amplified Bible (AMP) Copyright © 2015 by The Lockman Foundation
- Amplified Bible, Classic Edition (AMPC) Copyright © 1954, 1958, 1962, 1964, 1965, 1987 by The Lockman Foundation
- Holy Bible, New International Version®, NIV® Copyright ©1973, 1978, 1984, 2011 by Biblica
- Scripture quotations marked TPT are from The Passion Translation®. Copyright © 2017, 2018 by Passion & Fire Ministries, Inc. Used by permission. All rights reserved. ThePassionTranslation.com.
- The Message (MSG) Copyright © 1993, 2002, 2018 by Eugene H. Peterson
- New American Standard Bible (NASB) Copyright © 1960, 1962, 1963, 1968, 1971, 1972, 1973, 1975, 1977, 1995 by The Lockman Foundation

ImagineWhatCouldBe.com

Table of Contents

About the Author 4

1 / Deeply Rooted Faith, or Not 6

2 / Fully Persuaded Faith 10

3 / Help Thou Mine Unbelief 20

4 / Developing Faith 29

5 / In the Waiting 38

6 / God's Decisions 42

7 / Love 46

8 / The Importance of Words 60

9 / Speak What You Desire 71

10 / Word of God 80

11 / With Him 91

Prayer for Salvation 98

Appendix: Health that Wars Against Faith 99

About the Author

My wife and I live in California and have two grown children and four grandchildren. I spent many years in the financial world as a real estate and loan broker, specializing in construction financing.

I accepted Christ as a young boy, and decades later, came to a point in my life that I longed to know the Lord in a much deeper way. I wanted Him as my complete source, and to do that involved faith, a fully persuaded faith. The pursuit of developing faith became a passion for me, and this book is a result of that journey.

I also have an interest in the area of natural health. It began thirty-three years ago when I allowed God to redirect my life. I was able to kick my sugar addiction and walked away from the standard American diet. He placed in me a passion for natural health and the prevention of disease, and I've never looked back. As a result of my interest in health, I hold certifications as a health consultant and a plant-based chef.

But the greatest accomplishment of all, my name is written in the Lamb's Book of Life! God sees me, as He does you, as our destination. He has a plan for each of us to fulfill and it takes walking with Him, by faith.

As you and I pursue God and His will for our lives, and allow His possibilities to take root, we are blessed because we are in Christ!

Jesus is Lord,

David

You can learn more about David, at:

ImagineWhatCouldBe.com

Special Acknowledgement

I want to personally thank my wife for her contribution to making this book a reality. I love you, and so appreciate your talents in helping me organize and put this book together. I couldn't have done it without you!

1 / Deeply Rooted Faith, or Not

"When the Son of Man comes, will he find faith on the earth."
Luke 18:8 NIV.

It's a question that begs us to then ask of ourselves, *will He find me living in faith, fully persuaded?* A faith that is constant, consistent, and ever-present. A fully persuaded faith that believes God's Word will be personally performed in my life!

We can easily say we have faith in God and His Word, yet to believe beyond a shadow of doubt, in a fully persuaded fashion often eludes us.

What Christ accomplished through His scourging, hanging on the cross, and resurrection, is a finished, once-and-for-all work. And it is immense. Contained within His finished work is restoration with God the Father and victory over guilt, shame, and grief. It also includes provision for peace, joy, health, healing, wholeness, and abundant life.

Personally, there came a point in my life when I realized that though I loved the Lord, my faith in each of the finished works of Christ, and the promises of God's Word, were not deeply rooted in my heart. Instead, they were simply head knowledge. As troubles came, I did my best to trust God but it didn't take much to knock me over. My faith was far from developed.

So why is being fully persuaded such a struggle? For me, as a young child I developed several negative self-beliefs that plagued me for most of my life.

I felt in order to be good enough, and loved, I had to be perfect. I became very self-conscious, and as a result, moved quickly from being confident and out-going, to fearful and increasingly withdrawn, hiding in my own little shell from the world. At such a young age I wasn't emotionally able to handle how I felt, other than to default to a self-protective mechanism in order to cope with the world.

As the years passed, I developed a failure mentality, and struggled through life with this mindset. It became a default setting. I lived a life of inner struggle, depression, loneliness, and as a result, missed out on countless opportunities in every area of my life. I was consumed with the battle raging in my mind, and knew of no way to escape. And all this time I was a believer, raised in the church and attending regularly.

How could I ever expect to have a fully persuaded faith while living with these inner self-images? I was continually subject to anything that triggered these negative beliefs and was swallowed up in the power they held over me. Which is exactly what the enemy of my soul had set out to accomplish. Just as God is real, so is Satan. He had a calculated plan to ruin my life.

I lived for decades with no real direction, in a sea of fear and emotions. I tried to overcome these, but always crash landed. Then came a point where I was more determined than ever to succeed, and where God took me was to faith. So, I immersed myself in the journey and became a student of faith, a student of God's Word.

I read the accounts of those in the Bible who were recognized for their faith and why. I was also impressed, as I watched people of strong faith, and their certainty of God's Word and amazing victories that followed them. With a desire to grow, I read books and listened to messages on faith. I spent several years consumed with developing my faith. Since then, it's become a daily and lifelong endeavor.

Your story may be different than mine, but most people experience daily battles raging against their faith. So where is your faith right now?

Do you believe God is your provider and deliverer yet find yourself speaking *'maybe He will'*, or *'sometimes He does and sometimes He doesn't'*?

If it's the same Jesus, the same cross, and the same resurrection, why is it so easy for us to have faith at salvation for forgiveness of sin, but not for God's other promises given to us?

However, it's not only we today who struggle in this area. Consider the disciples who watched Jesus, listened, and spent a lot of personal time with Him. At one point Jesus said to Peter, *what little faith you have … why do you let doubt win?* Matthew 14:31 TPT.

God is Spirit and operates in the spiritual realm. His Word, wrapped in faith, brings forth things from the spiritual realm into the physical realm. His Word and promises originate in Him. In fact, John 1:3 tells us all created things came through Jesus. Hebrew 12:2 also tells us that *"Jesus* (is) *the author and finisher of our faith"* KJV. He is there in the beginning and will stand by you to see it through to the end.

So how do we move from head knowledge to getting it into the soil of our hearts? How do we prevent the busyness and the cares of life from robbing our faith? The rest of this book is devoted to finding answers to these questions so you can walk fully persuaded. I invite you to ask the Holy Spirit to speak Truth into the depths of your soul as we move forward.

2 / Fully Persuaded Faith

Fully persuaded faith is simply and powerfully receiving something as true based on God's Word. It knows Jesus is Lord and that God's Word is spiritual law and the only principles of true life. Faith is a fact, established in our heart, that we know God is able to perform His Word. Faith believes God's Word regardless of what we see, hear, or feel. It doesn't tell time, get embarrassed, is not timid, nor does it pay attention to the size of the obstacle, but believes regardless of circumstances. *"For with God nothing shall be impossible."* Luke 1:37 KJV.

Faith allows us to live in the fullness of the love, blessing, and provision of God because it doesn't believe God *can* perform His Word. It believes God *does* and *will* perform His Word. It takes possession of what God has already provided and has complete confidence in the integrity of His Word.

God's Kingdom depends on faith because *"**without** faith it is impossible* (not possible*) to please* (to be fully agreeable) *and be satisfactory to Him."* Hebrews 11:6 AMP.

The Greek word for *without* is 'choris'. Choris depicts someone who is *out of, or not in, a specific location*. God wants you to be in the specific location of faith, rather than in locations of worry, doubt, or unbelief.

The Word also tells us *"everything that does not come from faith is sin"*. Romans 14:23 NIV. We define sin as missing the mark. Thus, if we are not living by faith, we are missing the mark of the life God's wants us to live. Faith is trusting in the integrity of God and His Word, and enables us to walk with God.

Fully persuaded faith is also a deep conviction of the reality that God cannot lie, and that every answer, every manifestation of God's Word and His promises, and all the finished work of the cross, are found in Christ. Everything we need comes through Him. The laws and principles of God's Word never change. Uncompromised faith and love are the keys that unlock the doors so that the fullness of salvation can be experienced. We use faith to receive salvation, then we have to grow up. It takes fully persuaded faith to do so.

Too often we've been taught to believe *in* God, but faith believes *with* God. Fully persuaded faith is not a feeling. It is a decision, an uncompromised decision, to place our faith in Him, in His love, and in His faithfulness to His Word.

The Five Senses or God's Way

We live in a physical world, and it's quite natural for us to operate based on our five senses. These provide pleasure, protection, and help us function in our natural state. But we tend to believe things exist only when we are able to see, touch, smell, hear, or taste. By these, we verify whether something is true or not. But if we depend only on our senses, we can actually believe incorrectly and contradict God's Word. Natural or earthly facts, as we tend to interpret them, are not necessarily truth as seen through God's perspective.

Your diagnosis, symptoms, or circumstance may be facts but they are not necessarily truth. The facts are changeable, the truth of God's Word is not. In other words, God's truth trumps facts, and can change things in the natural realm. We must believe that the Word of God is truth, and our final authority.

"That your faith should not stand in the wisdom of men, but in the power of God." 1 Corinthians 2:5 KJV.

Sometimes you have to stand alone, or look the fool, because faith goes against human reasoning. You may be ridiculed if you choose to walk and talk in bold faith, trusting in the integrity of God's Word and the finished works of Christ.

But that's exactly what God is looking for - a person with extreme courage and determination to hold fast to His Word.

"For I am not ashamed of the gospel of Christ: for it is the power of God unto (that brings) *salvation to every one that believeth. For therein is the righteousness of God revealed from faith to faith: as it is written, the just shall live by faith."* Romans 1:16-17 KJV.

Fully persuaded faith moves us from receiving life *through* faith, to the power of living *by* faith.

The Connection

Faith is the connection to what has already been done. For example, if you needed a washing machine, and I purchased it for you and told you it's stored in my garage, you wouldn't continue asking. You would only need to receive what's already been bought and paid for. All of God's promises, including the purposes of your life, have already been ransomed and paid for. For that reason, when we focus our attention on the Word and the promises of God as our reality, it's not about getting God to do something, but rather a matter of receiving what has already been done, bought, and paid for. It's getting connected to the life of God's Word and His will. How do we get connected? We do so, by simply choosing to believe by exercising faith in His Word.

We can't trust who we don't know, but we do trust someone with whom we've spent time, and have a relationship. We begin learning how to use faith by getting to know our Lord, and finding out what God says in His Word. We discover what belongs to us (His will for our lives), and receive it by faith, despite what our five senses tell us.

All things have their root in and come from the spiritual realm before being manifested in the natural realm. How do we know that? God, who is Spirit, formed Creation. It was God's faith-filled spoken word that produced and created life. Man was made in God's image and God spoke or breathed the life of His spirit into him. We are spirit beings, housed in a physical body, and without a spirit the physical body would fall dead to the ground. Simply stated, the realm of the spirit is the source of all things natural because everything operates according to spiritual law. And the mechanism that connects us to what is happening in the spiritual realm is faith.

God's Word carries life, and when you receive and activate it through faith *it imparts true life into the very core of your being* (Proverbs 4:22 TPT).

"For the Word that God speaks is alive and full of power (making it active, operative, energizing, and effective)." Hebrews 4:12 AMP.

"By faith we understand that the universe was formed at God's command (by the word of God)*, so that what is seen was not made out of what was visible."* Hebrews 11:3 NIV.

Now Faith

The Word defines faith as *"the assurance (the confirmation, the title deed) of the things (we) hope for, being the proof of things (we) do not see and the conviction of their reality (faith perceiving as real fact what is not revealed to the senses)."* Hebrews 11:1 AMP.

The King James version states it as, *"Now faith is the substance of things hoped for, the evidence of things not seen."*

It's not yesterday's faith, but 'now' faith. Faith is always operating in the present moment, and Jesus is the author and the 'now' of our faith. In Him is the substance and evidence of all things today and tomorrow, because He is the finisher of our faith.

To be a Christian and walk in grace and experience the supernatural things of God, faith is not an option. When we know the will of God and pray in faith, knowing He hears us, we have what we pray for though the manifestation of it may not always be instant before our eyes.

"And this is the confidence that we have in him, that, if we ask any thing according to his will, he heareth us: And if we know that he hear us, whatsoever we ask, we know that we have the petitions that we desired of him." 1 John 5:14-15 KJV.

To be truly confident in God's Word means you walk in a level of constant expectancy because you can't separate what you are expecting from what actually happens.

That does not mean we dictate to God how something should be done, how it will look, or how long it should take. But it does mean we anticipate and stay joyful in the process. You Lord, are *"famous for great and unexpected acts; there's no end to Your surprises."* Job 5:9 MSG

But what about Mark 11:24, that says, *"Therefore I say unto you, What things soever ye desire, when ye pray, believe that ye receive them, and ye shall have them."* KJV.

God will not let you use His Word to violate it. What you believe for must be found in scripture. Though you can believe and proclaim anything you choose, you cannot pray for what the atonement of Christ did not provide. God's Word says that it is good for man to have a wife, but it doesn't say I can pray to have my neighbor's wife. God's Word addresses any issues in life, but you must align *what* you pray to His will. His will is in His Word. Pray the Word, and get His Word in your mouth.

When we see through the eyes of faith, we are calling those things that are not, as though they were. That is so powerful because faith will take us to our destination, and as it is manifested, faith becomes a living testimony of God's provision and blessing.

Shield of Faith

God has supplied us with heavenly weapons and armor. His Word, truth, righteousness, peace, salvation, and yes, faith.

In every battle of life, in all circumstances, faith is our shield of protection. It's what we use to clothe ourselves every day so that the enemy can't access our minds and lives. Think of it as a force field which cannot be penetrated.

"Take up the shield of faith, with which you can extinguish all the flaming arrows of the evil one." Ephesians 6:16 NIV.

16

Through our faith, we are also shielded by the mighty power of God, which is constantly guarding us.

"In his great mercy he has given us new birth into a living hope through the resurrection of Jesus Christ from the dead, and into an inheritance that can never perish, spoil or fade. This inheritance is kept in heaven for you, who through faith are shielded by God's power until the coming of the salvation that is ready to be revealed in the last time." 1 Peter 1:3-5 NIV.

Attend to My Word

The more attention we give to God's Word and the more we have in us, the more we can re-direct our faith from the natural things and reports of this world, to the assurance of things hoped for out of God's Word.

Blessed is the man who delights in the Word of God and meditates on it day and night (Psalms 1:1-2).

In Proverbs 4:20-23 we are told to *"Pay attention to what I say; turn your ear to my words. Do not let them out of your sight, keep them within your heart; for they are life to those who find them and health* (meaning medicine) *to one's whole body. Above all else, guard your heart* (with all diligence), *for everything you do flows from it* (the issues of life)." NIV.

We never have to question whether or not God honors His Word. In fact, our faith should soar at the power and life found in it, knowing that He magnifies His Word above all His name.

*"I will worship toward Your holy temple and praise Your name for Your loving-kindness and for Your truth and faithfulness; for You have exalted above all else Your name and Your word and You have **magnified Your word** above all Your name!"* Psalm 138:2 AMP.

For God not to respond to one of His promises would mean He would have to deny His name. He's not going to do that, thus we have full assurance that faith exercised in His Word, is established upon His righteousness.

"He remains true (faithful to His Word and His righteous character), for He cannot deny Himself." 2 Timothy 2:13 AMP.

No matter what the issues are in your life, God is waiting for you to step up and believe His Word with crazy, relentless faith. It's not about getting God to do something, it's about pursuing Him in relationship, with complete trust in Him and His Word and allowing Him to enrich your life with His finished works.

"Seek ye first the kingdom of God, and his righteousness; and all these things shall be added unto you." Matthew 6:23 KJV.

We can stand on the same instruction and promises the Lord gave to Joshua: *"Be strong and courageous. Do not turn from it to the right or to the left, that you may be successful wherever you go. Meditate on it day and night, so that you may be careful to do everything written in it. Then you will be prosperous and successful."* Joshua 1:7,8 NIV.

It is our faith, and being born of God, that allows us to overcome the world. *"For whatsoever is born of God overcometh the world: and this is the victory that overcometh the world, even our faith."* 1 John 5:4 KJV.

The Passion version states is simply, "You see, *every child of God overcomes the world, for our faith is the victorious power that triumphs over the world."*

The kind of faith we are speaking of, and the things ahead that we'll be discussing may seem radical, but that's what God is looking for. Despite anything we may be up against, we must reach a place of belief where the reality of the Word becomes more real than the problem. We can trust Him fully in any circumstance, knowing He is faithful to His Word.

We are at a pivotal point in the history of mankind, as well as in the church, and it's time to decide on which side of the fence we'll stand. The only way to stand with God is to remain in Him and His Word so that His Word becomes a living force in us rather than scriptural slogans.

The process of developing a fully persuaded faith is simply and powerfully receiving something as true based on God's Word, and acting on it. But we've all struggled and experienced times of uncertainty. Have you ever felt as though you have little or no faith? If so, we will see in the next chapter that it's probably not the amount of faith that's lacking.

3 / Help Thou Mine Unbelief

So often we feel that we lack enough faith. The disciples were no different. In Luke 17:5-6, they were feeling like that when they asked Jesus to increase their faith. Jesus responded by saying all they needed was faith the size of a tiny seed.

"And the apostles said unto the Lord, Increase our faith. And the Lord said, If ye had faith as a grain of mustard seed, ye might say unto this sycamine tree, Be thou plucked up by the root, and be thou planted in the sea; and it should obey you." Luke 17:6-7 KJV

Adding more faith to what they already had wasn't the issue. The problem wasn't so much a lack of faith, but the presence of too much doubt and unbelief. Like the man who *"cried out, and said with tears, Lord, I believe; help thou mine unbelief."* Mark 9:24 NIV.

Romans 12:3 tells us that we have been given a measure of faith. So, it's probably safe to say that it's never a lack of faith but rather the presence of unbelief that causes us to lose hope and expectation when we get our eyes off Jesus and the integrity of God's Word.

Walking in fully persuaded faith and into our spiritual provisions found in the promises of God, requires believing without doubt.

"For verily I say unto you, That whosoever shall say unto this mountain, Be thou removed, and be thou cast into the sea; and shall not doubt in his heart, but shall believe that those things which he saith shall come to pass; he shall have whatsoever he saith." Mark 11:23 KJV.

We have the cross and God's Word, which is His covenant. We are blessed. We live under grace and have the living Spirit of God inside us. Yet when issues of life raise their ugly heads, too often these issues and doubt are what dictate our responses rather than our belief in God's ability, His Word, and in what He has already accomplished.

When God brought the Israelites out of bondage in Egypt, His intention was for them to live in the Promised Land. But rather than trust in God, they complained and murmured against Him. They did not enter into His rest, which is trust and confidence in God's love and ability to care for them. Rather than speaking in agreement with life, the Israelites chose not to mix faith with God's Word and they spoke against it and died in the desert. They never entered the Promised Land due to the unbelief of their hearts. (Hebrews 4:6).

In another situation, the disciples were asked by a father to help his "lunatic" son, who was controlled by a demonic force. The disciples had previously been given the power to cast out demonic spirits (Matthew 10:1), yet they could not cure the boy (Matthew 17:15-16).

"Then Jesus answered and said, O faithless and perverse generation, how long shall I be with you? How long shall I suffer you? Bring him hither to me. And Jesus rebuked the devil; and he departed out of him: and the child was cured from that very hour". Matthew 17:17-18 KJV.

Later the disciples approached Jesus and asked why they couldn't cure the boy? Jesus flat out said, *"Because of your unbelief."* He continued by saying, all you need is faith the size of a mustard seed, and anything is possible. (Matthew 17:19-20).

There were also other situations. Instead of trusting, the disciples feared they were going to die when a terrible storm arose while they were out in a boat. Jesus responded by saying, *"Why are you so afraid? Haven't you learned to trust yet?"* Mark 4:40 TPT.

After experiencing firsthand, the feeding of the 5,000, the disciples once again seemed clueless when faced with 4,000 men to feed, plus women and children. When they questioned what to do, Jesus asked, *"Do you still not understand?"* Mark 8:21 NIV.

But when people came to Jesus with expectation and faith, the power of God moved. Speaking to a leper, Jesus said, *"Rise and go; your faith has made you well."* Luke 17:19 NIV.

"Daughter, because you dared to believe, your faith has healed you. Go with peace in your heart, and be free from your suffering!" Mark 5:34 TPT.

And in Mark 10:52, Jesus responded, *"Your faith heals you. Go in peace, with your sight restored."* TPT.

A Calloused Heart

Unbelief will grow when we ignore the Word or allow our hearts to become calloused or hardened. A calloused heart means we've become lukewarm, cold, or hardened to the things and voice of God, and that we consider the things of this world more than Him. Whether it's God's Word or a worldly desire, where we place our focus becomes the stronger attraction. Have our hearts become calloused so that we fail to remember all Jesus has done in our lives? Are we numbed to the fact that 2,000 years ago, Christ's complete and finished work redeemed us from the curse; from things connected to sin and death? And that we've been given *exceedingly great and precious promises*? (2 Peter 1:4).

Unless we view something as vitally important, we won't pursue it or think on it. Be honest with yourself. Is reading and meditating on God's Word a daily priority?

"For where your treasure is, there will your heart be also." Matthew 6:21 KJV. And if one's eye be single-minded and focused, *"thy whole body shall be full of light."* Matthew 6:22 KJV.

The following are a few things that will produce and keep us stuck in unbelief:

- Complaining (rather than trusting)
- Gossiping (foolish and idle words)
- Fear (which opposes faith)
- Lost hope (gets our eyes off Jesus)
- Judgment (not operating in love)
- Strife (confusion and every evil work)
- Negativity (criticism and pessimism)

Hebrews 3:12 says, *"Take heed, brethren, lest there be in any of you an evil heart of unbelief."* KJV.

Jesus also said, *"Pay careful attention to your hearts as you hear my teaching, for to those who have open hearts, even more revelation will be given to them until it overflows. And for those who do not listen with open hearts, what little light they imagine to have will be taken away."* Luke 8:18 TPT.

Hebrews 3 and 4 urge us when to act. *"Today if ye will hear his voice, Harden not your hearts."* Hebrews 3:7-8 and 4:7 KJV.

If you feel your heart has become hardened or calloused to the things of God and His Word, tell the Lord. Ask Him for a renewed zeal, and begin acting upon it by saying no to the world and giving more time to Him and His Word.

Expectation

If we say we believe, but don't expect, it's really unbelief. Have you ever asked God for something, or been prayed for, but deep down did not expect to receive? Most likely, we've all experienced this. But the Word says, *"make sure you ask empowered by confident faith without doubting that you will receive."* James 1:6 TPT. Expectation is something that is attached to faith, it's a natural response that comes with living by faith.

God's Word is His covenant, and it never fails, so we trust in His faithfulness to His Word and expect to receive.

"For we come to God in faith knowing that he is real and that he rewards the faith of those who give all their passion and strength into seeking him." Hebrews 11:6 TPT.

Fear-based

Doubt and worry are both fear-based, rather than faith-based responses. When we allow thoughts of doubt and worry to take root within us, that's when they become a problem. Fear undermines the promises and power of God because dwelling on problems keeps you from fulfilling God's purpose in your life. It detours your focus on the Lord and His Word. It will also cripple and hold you in bondage to wrong attitudes, habits, and behaviors that limit vision, goals, and dreams. Fear will always pull you over into the natural realm, causing you to believe only what you see and feel.

Fear is actually a form of faith, just faith in the wrong things. Faith in God is the opposite of fear. Fear will always move you in the direction of some form of death, while faith connects you to God's Kingdom realm of life.

Satan's spiritual kingdom is active upon the earth, and invoking fear is one of his main tactics. His playground is our mind. In fact, he will use any form of adversity to stir you up and steal your faith. He is a liar and a thief, and will always go after your thought life. Be alert, for something will continually show up in your life to get you to respond in some manner of faith.

If we fail to use the Word of God to cast down doubt, fear, or negative thoughts, they will become stronger. We don't want fears to infiltrate our mind. Satan works through fear, while God works through faith.

The next time unbelief, doubt, or fear of any kind begins to creep in and steal your ability to believe and praise God, remember that fear is opposing your faith. To cast down these vain imaginations and wrong thoughts, we use our mouth. Recently I read an account of a man who had been killed in an accident, taken up to heaven, and then sent back to finish his life. While in heaven, Jesus showed him that when people pray and speak in faith, using the name of Jesus, angelic forces appear, while demonic forces retreat. But, when doubt and unbelief are spoken, demonic forces not only appear, but become the dominating force.

Fear tolerated contaminates faith, while nourishing doubt and unbelief. But if we speak the answers to those things by declaring God's Word, fear will die for lack of nourishment.

While it's fear that opens doors and allows things we don't want to come in, such as torment, it's faith that shuts them out. We can choose to be highly developed in fear, or highly developed in faith. Place your confidence and trust in God, because *"With God all things are possible"* for those who believe. (Matthew 19:26)

Mark 4:14 tells us that when we hear and sow the Word into our hearts, know that Satan will immediately come to try to steal the Word. When we are moved more by what we see and feel, rather than by what God says, you can be certain that Satan will make a move to steal the Word and weaken your faith. At those times, we must rise up and begin speaking faith-filled words out loud that line up with God's Word. Faith and fear cannot occupy the same space at the same time; one will take precedence, while the other must go. The choice is ours.

In fact, in order to love the Lord and develop fully persuaded faith, you must stop dead anything that pulls you away from an intimate relationship of trust in the Lord and in His Word. Satan wants to distracts you and create doubt and fear. It must not be tolerated, but dealt with quickly, and not allowed to root itself. God is a jealous God (Exodus 34:14), and fiercely protective of you. You must be the same of Him.

Let's Make it Simple

Frequently, our belief is based on our performance rather than our trust in God's Word; in our efforts rather than His.

In John 14 Jesus explains the process of faith and belief. Jesus said, *"I do not say on My own initiative or authority, but the Father, abiding continually in Me, does His works."* John 14:10 AMP.

The process hasn't really changed. When we accept Christ, we are now in Him and He is in us. All we're required to do is to believe and trust, and do what God tells us to do, speak what He tells us to say, and then stand in faith on what He's already done. What to do and say is found in His Word and through being led by the Holy Spirit. The Holy Spirit does the work, but we are the ones called to stand and believe and proclaim God's Word in faith.

The finished work of Christ redeemed us. We are positioned differently because of what He has done. We've been given authority to speak and take spiritual dominion over our homes and workplaces, over unclean spirits, and mountains that arise in our lives.

Though God authorized the operation of the earth to us, it's not *our* power but *His* that does the work. We're just called to stand and be the mouthpiece of faith.

4 / Developing Faith

From a young age I remember going to church every Sunday. I suppose throughout all those years the verse, *"the just shall live by faith"* Galatians 3:11 KJV, was preached, or at least mentioned from time to time. And if it was, it never was taught so that it deposited anything in me.

I understood that God had given me a measure of faith, the Word tells us that in Romans 12:3. But as I stated before, it wasn't about getting more faith, but developing the faith I had been given. That was the key, and became my focus. The potential for growth contained within my measure of faith was right in front of me all the time.

So, just as we must daily feed the physical body food for nourishment and strength, we must continually feed our spirit and soul the Word of God for faith to develop and grow stronger. We do this by tuning our ears and hearts toward the words of Christ, and hearing about the faithfulness of God.

"Faith comes from hearing, and hearing by the word of Christ." Romans 10:17 NASB.

Hearing about His nature, His character, what He has done, all that He is, and all He provides develops our faith as we walk with Him. When we come into agreement with a promise of God, we begin with our measure of faith, even if it's only the size of a mustard seed. But to develop faith, we don't just think about the promise and hope it comes to pass, and we don't respond based on feelings. We make a quality decision to believe.

When we make a quality decision to exercise faith and allow it to grow in us, we first have to decide whether or not we believe God. Faith is a quality decision on which you base your life, knowing God is fully capable to perform His Word. We don't yield to discouragement, or allow ourselves to give up and quit.

We realize that all finished works of Christ have been made available to us. These are in our covenant of salvation, but we have to actively pursue them by developing our faith.

And time is not the issue because we know that God's timing is perfect and He is faithful to perform His Word. He only requires our faith. His answer begins the moment you activate your faith.

Abraham understood this, and it changed his life. He saw things differently, he spoke differently, and his actions aligned with God. He embraced what God had spoken to him: *"His* (Abraham) *action cooperated with his faith and by his action faith found its full expression?"* James 2:22 TPT.

James 2:26 tells us, *"For just as a human body without the spirit is a dead corpse, so faith without the expression of good works is dead!"* TPT. And in verse 1, James tells us, *"Even so faith, if it hath not works, is dead, being alone"* KJV. The Passion translation states it this way, *"faith that doesn't involve action is phony."*

What does faith with action look like? First and foremost, it begins by actively aligning our thoughts in agreement with God's Word. The first action is to simply believe God! Then we allow its full expression by the words we speak and any corresponding actions, or works.

Abraham believed and was fully persuaded when God told him he would have a son, though he was 100 years old at the time, and his wife Sarah was beyond child bearing. They were to name their son Isaac, and through his lineage, Abraham would be the father of many nations. When his son, Isaac, was around 18-20 years of age, God told Abraham to sacrifice him. Abraham did not hesitate. He acted in faith, believing that God would either deliver Isaac or would bring him back to life because of what was promised.

"Abraham's faith made it logical to him that God could raise Isaac from the dead." Hebrews 11:19 TPT.

We know that God provided a lamb to be sacrificed instead, but through Abraham's faith actions, he was considered to be righteous. Because Abraham's thoughts and actions aligned with God, his life was richly blessed.

Another example of faith and action, was the centurion discussed in Matthew 8. The centurion approached Jesus, asking for His help. *"Lord,"* he said, *"my servant lies at home paralyzed, suffering terribly."* The centurion, being over many soldiers, understood what it meant to have authority. He had faith in the authority of Jesus' words and said that if Jesus would simply speak healing, he knew his servant would be healed. And that's exactly what happened. Jesus said of the centurion, *"Truly I tell you, I have not found anyone in Israel with such great faith."* NIV. It was the centurion's fully persuaded faith and his action of seeking out Jesus that caused Jesus to heal the centurion's servant.

Belief Without Doubt

A person who is unsure, doubtful, and indecisive believes one minute and doubts the next. Wavering leaves a person unstable and in no condition to receive from the Lord. But firm belief causes one to receive.

"But let him ask in faith, nothing wavering. For he that wavereth is like a wave of the sea driven with the wind and tossed. For let not that man think that he shall receive any thing of the Lord." James 1:6-7 KJV.

"Therefore I tell you, whatever you ask for in prayer, believe that you have received it, and it will be yours.". Mark 11:24 KJV.

When we are within His will, in covenant relationship, standing on the promises of His Word, and knowing that He is

32

faithful to His Word, we can rest in complete assurance. As He told Jeremiah, *"You have seen well, for I am (actively) watching over My word to fulfill it."* Jeremiah 1:12 AMP.

What part of His Word does He watch over? All of it! That includes the Word we are trusting Him to fulfill and speaking from our lips.

The following example expresses well the difference between doubt and belief, how much Word a person has within them, and whether or not they take ownership of it.

Two individuals exercised their faith for employment. One stood on a promise and the other did not. In the waiting period, whenever asked if they had received a job, one would state, "Not yet, but jobs are hard to find in this economy." The other responded, "Yes, I've got my job; I just don't know where it is yet." Which individual was actually believing that God and His Word, mixed with their faith, was actively working on their behalf? It's the one who could see the job through the eyes of faith.

With God there is no such thing as 'no' for an answer when it comes to His Word and His promises. *All of God's promises in Christ Jesus are yes and amen* (2 Corinthians 1:20). All the promises of God's Word find their fullness in and through Christ. The answer may look different than you expected, but you trust in it, for He knows what is for your best.

And let's not forget, Jesus is not only the author of our faith, but the finisher. He sees us through to the very end.

"Being confident of this, that he who began a good work in you will carry it on to completion until the day of Christ Jesus." Philippians 1:6 NIV.

So how do we not waiver? It's about moving past intellectual knowledge, and spending time in the Word. It is not considering the problem, but the promise. It's developing a confidence in the Lord through relationship, and knowing He is faithful to His Word.

"In spite of being nearly one hundred years old when the promise of having a son was made, his (Abraham's) *faith was so strong that it could not be undermined by the fact that he and Sarah were incapable of conceiving a child."* Romans 4:19 TPT.

After we release our faith, the Word says, *"Cast not away therefore your confidence, which hath great recompence of reward."* Hebrews 10:35 KJV. In other words, don't lose your bold, courageous faith, and confidence in God's Word. Your faith will be rewarded! For *"The just shall live by faith."* Hebrews 10:38 KJV.

If God said it, we believe it. Jesus Himself said, *"Have faith in God."* Mark 11:22 KJV.

We know that if we drop something it will fall to the ground. It's the law of gravity. In the same way, we must be equally sure of God's Word. We don't question gravity, and we shouldn't question God's Word, but rather work in conjunction with it through faith.

Praise and Thanksgiving

Praise and thanksgiving are an integral part of developing faith. Regardless of the circumstances, Abraham praised God, and so should we.

"And because he (Abraham) *was mighty in faith and convinced that God had all the power needed to fulfill his promises, Abraham glorified God!"* Romans 4:21 TPT.

David even instructed his soul to bless and praise God:

"Bless the LORD, O my soul: and all that is within me, bless his holy name. Bless the LORD, O my soul, and forget not all his benefits:

- *Who forgives all your sins*
- *Heals all your diseases*
- *Who redeems your life from the pit*
- *Crowns you with love and compassion*
- *Who satisfies your desires with good things so that your youth is renewed like the eagle's.* Psalms 103:1-5 KJV and NIV.

Being thankful, and allowing praise to continually come forth from our mouths diminishes unbelief. When it comes to holding on to a promise, praise also keeps faith active and operative in our lives. Though no one else can yet see the manifestations of what you are praising and thanking God for, you see them through the Word of God and the eye of faith. Remember, faith is calling and seeing those things that are not as though they were. It's seeing the end from the beginning.

When we reach a point where the Word so overwhelms us, praise becomes a natural part of who we are. It will cause you to stop in your tracks, being so overwhelmed with emotion and awe of God's goodness, and the magnitude of who He is. Unbelief is removed from the equation, and belief and faith begin to blossom within you.

Praise is not just singing a song in church. Though singing can be an expression of it, praise is our daily communication with God, through our prayers, thoughts, words, and actions. It's putting our life on display.

Whether you dance before the Lord, quietly rejoice, or praise Him as you fulfill your responsibilities at work or home, the devil won't know what to do with you. Praise is warfare as we stand living a life of unmovable faith. The impact that comes from this type of praise causes demonic spirits to flee. It's this type of praise that takes us from experience to experience, from glory to glory.

Assignment

Faith develops and grows by using it, so give your measure of faith an assignment. If you have a current issue in your life, find a promise or verse from the Bible to stand on; one that addresses the issue, and clearly shows you God's will. Practice resting in God for resolutions to any issue. Exercise your faith muscle by praying it aloud to the Lord. Thank Him for His resolution. Whether the answer comes in a day, a week, or in a different season of your life, never back down from your confession.

What if your mind wants to wander over to doubt or worry regarding the situation? How do you exercise your faith? Choose to believe in the promise and the Promise Keeper. Practice resting in Him by praying the verse and thanking Him for the answer to come. When you are able to rest in His love and faithfulness, peace will emerge. It's often in this type of peace that He is able to do His best work in our lives.

5 / In the Waiting

When a person signs with a contractor to build a home, immediately things begin happening. Weeks and months may go by, as the land sits vacant, but it is not an indicator of inactivity. Behind the scenes, plans must be drawn and applications submitted to obtain a building permit. We may not see all that is taking place, but one day, manifestation begins to appear – a foundation is poured and framing begins. As things continue to progress, the result will be the completion of a home. This is not unlike God's Kingdom.

In Mark 4:26-29 we see this progression at work.

Jesus said: *"God's kingdom realm is like someone spreading seed on the ground. He goes to bed and gets up, day after day, and the seed sprouts and grows tall, though he knows not how. All by itself it sprouts, and the soil produces a crop; first the green stem, then the head on the stalk, and then the fully developed grain in the head. Then, when the grain is ripe, he immediately puts the sickle to the grain, because harvest time has come."* TPT.

When we choose to stand in faith, spiritual forces are immediately activated. Just like the farmer who plants a seed. Though he cannot see what's happening below the surface of the soil, he knows that the principles of growth are in play. He can't see the germination, the roots being sent downward, nor the sprout making its way upward to the topsoil. But he has faith in the seed's ability to sprout and grow.

When we have faith, without doubt, we understand that things are taking place in the spiritual realm. Though we can't see all that's happening, we know that life-producing activity is taking place because God is at work. The Holy Spirit is actively involved, and even angels may be sent on assignment to bring it to pass because they harken to the Word of God, which we confess and stand on.

Patience

When you sign up to be a person of faith and believe regardless of what you see or feel, you will need to employ patience. You may see quick results, but more often, when you decide to stand and believe for something in faith, as the farmer does with his seed, you must be patient.

God's word says that the trying or proving of our faith brings forth endurance and patience, and that we need to allow patience to have her perfect, complete work. (James 1:3-4)

The devil comes to **try** your faith and get you to waiver and doubt. But when you refuse to move, you **prove** your faith, allowing patience to have its perfect way.

Though Jesus already did the work to make all God's promises available to us, Satan will always come and try to steal the Word in order to get you so discouraged in doubt and unbelief, that you abandon faith. If you allow that, he becomes the finisher of your faith, rather than Jesus.

God's Word never fails. His Word always works. If it doesn't work, then why waste our time believing it? We should go find something else to stake our life on.

But as for me and my house, we know it works and will actively stand in strength, in absolute trust and confidence in His power, wisdom, and goodness.

Patience is not passive, but an active force of strength that understands there is a process involved, and knows success is inevitable.

Patience is active faith, and will wear down the enemy. In 1 Timothy 6:12, we are instructed to *"Fight the good fight of faith."* NKJV. Together, faith with patience will fight, even with violent pursuit, to see the promise of God manifest.

When the devil sees what you're made of, that you are serious about enforcing the Word of God, he'll give up and leave. Victory is yours.

It's called endurance, and may be the best description of patience. The Word tells us in James 1:3-4 that when your faith is put to the test and you refuse to be moved, *"it stirs up power within you to endure all things. And then as your endurance grows even stronger it will release perfection into every part of your being until there is nothing missing and nothing lacking."* TPT.

When you decide to stand in the face of opposition and not back down, God also comes alongside with His supernatural endurance. It's no longer a question of whether or not you are going to win. It's just a matter of when. In fact, you've already won because you choose to stand from a place of victory found in Him.

"So don't lose your bold, courageous faith, for you are destined for a great reward!" Hebrews 10:35 TPT.

Victory only comes in the standing. Standing is fully persuaded faith.

You can be *"confident of this, that he who began a good work in you will carry it on to completion until the day of Christ Jesus."* Philippians 1:6 NIV.

Whether His promise comes quickly or takes time, we devote ourselves to Him, follow His direction, and employ patience, knowing He is actively positioning things for our benefit and success!

> *"So don't allow your hearts to grow dull or lose your enthusiasm, but follow the example of those who fully received what God has promised because of their strong faith and patient endurance."*
> Hebrews 6:12 TPT.

6 / God's Decisions

I mentioned previously that I was taught to believe in God, but not how to develop my faith nor how to believe *with* God. I want to share something now that is so powerful, you can base your entire life on it and live in victory and abundance through any trial.

The promises in the Bible, and the plan of salvation, **were God's ideas and His decisions**. He is the great initiator. God decided there would be a plan of redemption. It was His idea to send Jesus to the cross so we could be redeemed. It was His decision that Jesus bear our sins and grief, and carry our sorrow. Jesus' chastisement was for our peace. His stripes were for our healing, and it was He who came to give us abundant life. Those were not man's ideas. There is no church or pastor who came up with them. It was God Himself. It was His will.

God has complete faith in His own words, and the fact that all those were His ideas and His decisions, guarantees their outcomes to those who come into agreement with Him and His Word. They are available to us through Christ, through grace. It is absolute truth that God's Word, His promises, and whatever He tells you to do, He has already provided everything to secure its outcome.

It's God's truth. But is it your truth?

To make it your truth, you need to come into agreement with God. You make a quality decision of faith about those things. Quality decisions are decisions of certainty, of faith, by which you live your life. A quality decision believes in what God has already decided is a no-lose proposition. For example, when you decided to believe Jesus is the Son of God as the only Savior of the world, you made a quality decision. There is a spiritual response that takes place when we agree with God. He responds to that kind of engaged faith by immediately putting things in motion in the spiritual realm. He's always ready to back up His Word. It's God expressing His love to us.

How do you know when you've made a quality decision in faith? It's when your actions and words line up with that decision. If your actions and words don't line up, you know the decision is not one of quality, nor of engaged faith. If you believe God is faithful, that He is your provider, and will see you through any trial, you don't complain, wallow in worry, nor take your eyes off Him and His promises. Instead, you continue to believe and speak what God's Word says He will provide. You must see through the eyes of faith to live by quality decisions.

Jesus gives us an example of how to make a quality decision in Mark 11:22-23: *"Have faith in God. For verily I say unto you, That whosoever shall say unto this mountain, Be thou removed, and be thou cast into the sea; and shall not doubt in his heart, but shall believe that those things which he saith shall come to pass; he shall have whatsoever he saith."* KJV.

Jesus was telling us to believe God with unwavering faith and speak to the issue at hand. He didn't say anything about having doubting thoughts, but He did tell us not to doubt in our hearts. Though we don't want doubt, everyone experiences doubt (fear, worry) from time to time. But God's Word tells us to cast down anything contrary to His Word, and take every thought captive to the obedience of Christ. In doing so, we protect our hearts.

"We can demolish every deceptive fantasy that opposes God and break through every arrogant attitude that is raised up in defiance of the true knowledge of God. We capture, like prisoners of war, every thought and insist that it bow in obedience to the Anointed One." 2 Corinthians 10:5 TPT.

We take ownership of something when we begin to focus and dwell on it, and begin speaking in agreement with it. If doubt isn't cast down and we choose to dwell on that instead, we will end up speaking it, which transfers it from our heads to our hearts. At that point we've let go of faith.

But by using faith, believing in the integrity of God and His love for us, we shall have what we say. And to pray in this manner, we must know God's will. We can and should know His will because the Word tells us so. *"Wherefore be ye not unwise, but understanding what the will of the Lord is."* Ephesians 5:17 KJV.

Inquire of God, dig into His Word and stand in agreement with it. Speak to the mountain and begin thanking and praising Him for what He is doing.

You can rest in your confession of faith in His Word, because you didn't write the Bible, He did. You didn't put spiritual laws and principles into action, He did. Which means it's His job to perform His Word, as we place our faith in Him. This is God's nature, to watch over His Word: *"for I am watching to see that my word is fulfilled."* Jeremiah 1:12 NIV.

We have been given the measure of His faith to live by. When we exercise it, as a quality decision of belief in line with His established decisions, He completes His work in our lives. It's living a life of faith based on His decisions, not man's wisdom. The justified are called to live by faith.

7 / Love

Back in the 1960's the Beatles made famous the saying, *All You Need is Love*. It was a phrase in a song that filled the radio airwaves. Throughout history poets, philosophers, and self-proclaimed saviors have also stated the same but missed the most important ingredient, the source of that love.

God doesn't have love, He is love (1 John 4:8), as He is also holy, just, and faithful. His love is immense, because He is immense. His love has no limits nor boundaries because He is infinite and eternal. God created us in His likeness and image. At the core of a believer's spirit being is love in its purest form because God dwells there.

The Creator of the entire universe wired and designed us for love. To speak or act in any other fashion, goes against the very fabric of our design.

"For God hath not given us the spirit of fear; but of power, and of love, and of a sound mind." 2 Timothy 1:7 KJV.

Anything other than acting and speaking in love confuses the body, the brain, and cellular structures. It causes chemical imbalances and contributes to chronic physical and mental diseases.

On the flip side, because we are designed in love, every fiber of our being - our brain, proteins, neurological circuits, and cellular structures are designed to respond favorably to love. Our body, mind, and brain operate at a high level when we conduct our lives according to God's design to love. To put in simple terms, if you want to live an extraordinary life, love as Jesus did.

Jesus, the Fulfillment of the Law

When Jesus walked this earth He said, *"I give you now a new commandment: Love each other just as much as I have loved you."* John 13:34 TPT.

At the time Jesus spoke this, people were living under the law, but He came as its fulfillment, instructing in the ways of love.

"Love does no wrong to one's neighbor (it never hurts anybody). *Therefore love meets all the requirements and is the fulfilling of the Law."* Romans 13:10 AMP.

To operate effectively in the Kingdom of God in faith requires that we fulfill the commandment of love. It begins by not only recognizing how much God loves us, but believing it!

Many of us struggle with accepting His love. Without this acceptance it is difficult to completely trust and have faith in Him and in all He wants to do for us.

Our life experiences with humanity often teach us to fear, doubt, and question. Many of us have suffered abuse or developed a poor self-image, feeling as though we are not good enough, resulting in a life of struggle and disappointments. Some of us still live with the memory of a sin, and stay in guilt or shame. As a result, we pull back from life and live at a level far less than our God-given potential.

Whether it is a sin we've committed, or a bad experience in our past, the memory of these can be more detrimental than the actual acts. They will beat on us, keep us locked up emotionally, or cause us to carry anger and unforgiveness. It's a form of death, and can be a huge roadblock to living a life of faith which includes the ability to discern correctly and experience freedom found in Christ.

If this is you, then the issue of His love for you needs to be settled once and for all. You are saved by the grace of God, not by anything you've done, how good you are, or what others have said about you. He loves you as you are, not as you should be.

"He chose us to be his very own, joining us to himself even before he laid the foundation of the universe! Because of his great love, he ordained us, so that we would be seen as holy in his eyes with an unstained innocence." Ephesians 1:4 TPT.

"This is love: not that we loved God, but that he loved us and sent his Son as an atoning sacrifice for our sins." 1 John 4:10 NIV. Every time we miss the mark, in Christ we are forgiven.

"Christ has now reconciled you (to God) in His physical body through death, in order to present you before the Father holy and blameless and beyond reproach." Colossians 1:22 AMP.

You can be assured of His love because He redeemed you before you sinned, in fact, before you were even born.

"For this is how much God loved the world - he gave his one and only, unique Son as a gift. So now everyone who believes in him will never perish but experience everlasting life." John 3:16 TPT.

Romans 8:1 *says, "There is therefore now no condemnation to them which are in Christ Jesus."* KJV. 'Now' isn't a few minutes ago. 'Now' is in the present moment. It doesn't matter what you've done. Right *'now'* there is no condemnation towards you. You are loved and set free.

We are His Children and Heirs

"See what an incredible quality of love the Father has shown to us, that we would (be permitted to) *be named and called and counted the children of God!"* 1 John 3:1 AMP.

Upon believing in Jesus as Savior, your spirit became filled with the Godhead (1 Corinthians 3:16). His love found its ultimate destination in you. When Christ was raised from the dead and returned back to the Father, the Word tells us, you were raised with Him (Ephesians 2:6), and are now spiritually seated in heavenly places with Jesus, positionally placed with Him in a place of victory.

Consider the story of Shadrach, Meshach, and Abednego. Because they worshiped God, the king bound and threw them into a blazing fiery furnace. In Daniel 3:25-27, the king said, *"Look! I see four men walking around in the fire,* **unbound** *and unharmed, and*

49

*the fourth looks like a son of the gods. Nebuchadnezzar then approached the opening of the blazing furnace and shouted, "Shadrach, Meshach and Abednego, servants of the Most High God, come out! Come here! So Shadrach, Meshach and Abednego came out of the fire … the fire had not harmed their bodies, their robes were not scorched, and there was **no smell of fire on them**"* NIV.

God's love and grace have already overcome the fires of your life, and have freed you. You are unbound from your past, and there is no smell of sin or guilt on you. Your past no longer defines you. You are a new creature in Christ because under the covenant of salvation and grace, you received the adoption as a son or daughter (Romans 8:15). You are an heir of God and a joint heir with Jesus (Romans 8:17).

In Christ you have been given a firm foundation on which to build your life. Just imagine, you were a chosen word from the mouth of God. He knows your name, and your life will not be void of goodness, but rather you will accomplish what He has destined you for.

What kind of love makes you an heir of God and joint heir with Jesus? What kind of love makes you destined with a purpose? It's His amazing love for you. You have been greatly elevated by God's love.

He takes great pleasure in blessing you, because He loves you so much. *"The Lord is great, and He delights in the prosperity of his servant."* Psalm 35:27 TPT.

There is nothing that you have done or experienced that God's love and His forgiveness does not cover. You are amazingly loved.

As Much as Jesus

Did you know that God the Father loves you just as much as He loves Jesus? Jesus said, *"And that the world may know that thou hast sent me, and hast loved them, as thou hast loved me* (Jesus).*"* John 17:23 KJV. Or stated another way, *"For they will see that you love each one of them with the same passionate love that you have for me."* TPT.

Sometimes I think our own head knowledge causes us to miss the immenseness and the type of love of which we are speaking. Love isn't a feeling, but a Person. God doesn't have to conjure up a feeling of love. It is one of His continual, never-ending attributes. Everything in your life, and your relationship with Him is engulfed by Him, His love, and His faithfulness.

"Neither death, nor life, nor angels, nor principalities, nor powers, nor things present, nor things to come, Nor height, nor depth, nor any other creature, shall be able to separate us from the love of God, which is in Christ Jesus our Lord." Romans 8:38-39 KJV.

You can believe His promises. You are forgiven and free from the bondage of sin. You are redeemed from the power and entirety of the curse and have the fullness of His blessing before you.

"Because his heart was focused on the joy of knowing that you would be his, he endured the agony of the cross." Hebrews 12:2 TPT. Wow, you are that loved and special to Him!

Because God loves you so much, you can truly rest within the storms of life. **His love leaves no doubt that you can believe and stand in faith on His Word**. It's His love that cares for you, protects you, and secures you. It's life-producing. It is unconditional, bountiful, and ever encompassing.

Why would anyone not want to develop a close relationship, with someone who loves them that much?

Forgiveness

In living by faith, we constantly have circumstances in our lives where we have the opportunity to live out our ability to love.

"All that matters now is living in the faith that is activated and brought to perfection by love." Galatians 5:6 TPT.

One of the key components that reveals whether or not we are perfected in love, is our ability to forgive. Faith will not work in an unforgiving heart because we are not operating in love.

"What things soever ye desire, when ye pray, believe that ye receive them, and ye shall have them. And when ye stand praying, forgive, if ye have ought against any." Mark 11:24-25 KJV.

Walking in love and operating in faith often begins with forgiving others, as well as ourselves. We no longer have to be held hostage to guilt for something we've done, nor to anger towards another for what they did. Don't ever allow Satan to bring up your past or put any condemnation on you again. You are completely forgiven and free from your past. God's grace has completely cleansed you from your mistakes. Because we are forgiven and so deeply loved, God wants us to extend the same grace to others.

"Be gentle and forbearing with one another and, if one has a difference (a grievance or complaint) against another, readily pardoning each other; even as the Lord has (freely) forgiven you, so must you also (forgive)." Colossians 3:13 AMP.

We forgive because it's God's design for us. It's a component of love. Not only does forgiveness bring restoration and closure, but it frees us from pain, bitterness, and a victim mentality.

To stay in either guilt or unforgiveness destroys the soul (mind, will, and emotions), and corrupts our ability to walk in love and faith. Staying in judgment or unforgiveness of another, and becoming bitter and jealous are all forms of self-pride and block our ability to hear properly from God.

"And make sure no one lives with a root of bitterness (resentment) *sprouting within them which will only cause trouble and poison the hearts of many."* Hebrews 12:15 TPT.

"So wherever jealousy and selfishness are uncovered, you will also find many troubles and every kind of meanness." James 3:16 TPT.

But, extending love through forgiveness is a form of extending mercy. Just as God extends mercy to you, you conform to His nature by doing the same. It gives victory over a judgmental heart.

"So we must both speak and act in every respect like those who are destined to be tried by the perfect law of liberty (law of love), *and remember that judgment is merciless for the one who judges others without mercy. So by showing mercy you take dominion over judgment!"* James 2:12-13 TPT.

When it comes to developing your faith, if you don't have mercy for another, your faith is dead because *"faith without the expression of good works is dead!"* James 2:26 TPT. Forgiveness and mercy are good works of living by faith.

And, let's face it, unforgiveness is a form of strife and where strife is there is confusion and every evil work (James 3:16). The very moment you enter into strife, faith falters and your ability to rest in Christ is not there.

So, when strife begins to rise up, and judgment or bitterness want to react, choose to respond instead. Responding takes thought and strength. It carefully considers what to say and allows you to responsibly respond in love. Just like you can build up a strong physical muscle, you can choose to forgive and build up the strength of your forgiveness muscle.

Lastly, we've heard it said that unforgiveness is like drinking poison and hoping the other person will die. To act in unforgiveness damages the brain by creating physical structures that keep us from being able to mentally function correctly. It causes inflammation and releases harmful chemicals, whereas forgiveness and love do just the opposite.

Unforgiveness produces bitterness, which is not of God. It is one of many evils. When we resolve any bitterness towards another, the body's ability to heal and function dramatically increases. Coming from a place of love and forgiveness is *"health to your body (your marrow, your nerves, your sinews, your muscles—all your inner parts), and refreshment (physical well-being) to your bones."* Proverbs 3:8 AMP. The body proves God's Word.

Offense

When we take offense to something someone has done or said, it's human nature to stand in judgment and develop ill feelings toward them. When you are offended, immediately recognize it for what it is, and how the devil would love to use it to take you off your course of faith, by responding in love. Rise above it and take the high road. Forgive. Let it go and move on.

Consider this: If someone wants to hand you a box and you refuse to take it, who has possession of the box? The person who holds the box, right? If someone offends you and you refuse to receive it, it stays with them. The temptation for unforgiveness or judgment cannot take root within you. The more you walk in love, and learn to not be offended by others, the more you will walk in freedom. As you walk in the freedom of His grace, in full trust in Him, your perspective and ability to walk in joy and confidence gets stronger. And you begin to see others through the eyes of Christ.

And besides, the Word tells us to never return insult for insult, but rather to bless the other person, which results in our inheriting a blessing from God (1 Peter 3:9 AMP).

To live above being offended is a choice we make.

Perfected Love

Perfected love could be summed up as living your life in such a manner that your words and actions are expressed through love.

"There is no fear in love, but perfect love casteth out fear: because fear hath torment (fear of punishment or judgment). *He that feareth is not made perfect in love."* 1 John 4:18 KJV.

I remember a number of years ago saying and doing something that hurt someone who trusted me. Later, as I looked back upon those moments, I had to ask myself, 'who was that person?' My ungodly and unloving responses were birthed from being in a place of fear. Satan works very hard and cunningly to

56

keep us in fear. He wants us to live with victim mentalities. He wants to keep us in a state of stress and anxiety, fill with worried thoughts about the future.

Of course, I repented for my behavior and for allowing my trust in fear to be greater than my trust in God. We must never forget, we have the Word of God, His Spirit, His love, and a covenant, which says God will never leave us nor fail us (Hebrews 13:5). He is always there to comfort and to guide us.

Developing faith and perfected love is what Christ expects. In fact, we are commanded to love and to forgive; these are not options. *"And do not grieve the Holy Spirit of God, with whom you were sealed for the day of redemption. Get rid of all bitterness, rage and anger, brawling and slander, along with every form of malice. Be kind and compassionate to one another, forgiving each other, just as in Christ God forgave you."* Ephesians 4:30-32 NIV.

To express love or forgiveness is an act of the will. It's a choice that requires action. And in anything God says to do, He provides the means and the strength by which to complete it. As we choose to forgive, judgmental thoughts disappear, allowing greater understanding, love, and mercy to be extended to others.

But, if you still have trouble forgiving another, you may need to forgive by faith. This means that you first make a quality decision to forgive. Then speak and act in accordance with your decision. Refuse to speak anything negative about the other person or rehearse in your mind the incident. Pray for them. If appropriate, look for opportunities to bless them in word or acts of kindness. Many times, the act of blessing the other person with a gift or kind words will break the power of unforgiveness.

If feelings of unforgiveness continue to rise inside you, remember that emotions begin with thoughts. Come against those thoughts in faith, and cast them down. Speak out loud, *"I have forgiven that person by an act of my will, in faith. I'm not moved by these feelings because I don't live by my emotions. I live by the Word of God"*. If you'll continue this, your feelings will change. It may not happen overnight, as with many things we do by faith, but eventually they do change. God will honor your faith and efforts. Psst ... and do wonders for your emotional and physical health.

Power of Love Summed Up

We have established that faith works by love, which is to say, it begins by how much we believe God loves us.

Living by faith is believing in His unchangeable Word and embracing the fullness of His love. The love God has for us is so intense that He is eager for us to experience spiritual blessings and the riches of His glory.

"All that matters now is living in the faith that is activated and brought to perfection by love." Galatians 5:6 TPT.

The complete package of salvation is founded on His love. In fact, the Word tells us that of faith, hope, and love, love is the greatest (1 Corinthians 13:13). And rightly so, because faith working through love is foundational in the Kingdom of God (Galatians 5:6).

Out of love flow character and the fruits of the Spirit: happiness, joy, peace, kindness, gentleness, self-control, hope, and patience.

It's a complete circle of love, from Him to us, because He first loved us. Then from us to others, and back to Him.

Yes, in His love lies eternal hope. Love produces an abundant life and has the power to heal us emotionally and physically.

As we close out this chapter, my prayer for you is found in Ephesians 3:16-19:

"I pray that he would unveil within you the unlimited riches of his glory and favor until supernatural strength floods your innermost being with his divine might and explosive power.

Then, by constantly using your faith, the life of Christ will be released deep inside you, and the resting place of his love will become the very source and root of your life. You will be empowered to discover the great magnitude of the astonishing love of Christ in all its dimensions.

How deeply intimate and far-reaching is his love! How enduring and inclusive it is! Endless love beyond measurement that transcends our understanding ... this extravagant love pours into you until you are filled to overflowing with the fullness of God!" TPT. Amen

8 / The Importance of Words

Another contributing factor to developing fully persuaded faith, is to understand how and why the words you speak have a major impact on what you experience in life. In fact, your thoughts and the words you speak point you in the direction of your destiny. They also tell you a lot about your level of faith.

Why are the words you speak so important? Because words carry identity and frame the thoughts you hold in your heart. We live in a word-based society. It all began when God formed all of creation with His faith-filled words.

"Through faith we understand that the worlds were framed by the word of God, so that things which are seen were not made of things which do appear." Hebrew 11:3 KJV. *"And God said, Let there be light: and there was light."* Genesis 1:3 KJV.

God spoke words that were not as though they were, into physical manifestation. All created things came forth from His mouth, from the spiritual realm into the physical realm. We are surrounded by the power and influence of God's words.

We have God's spoken words, His written words, and the living Word Himself, Jesus Christ.

"In the beginning was the Word and the Word was with God and the Word was God." John 1:1 KJV. *"And the Word was made flesh, and dwelt among us."* John 1:14 KJV.

Satan's Plan

Satan is also under the same system. This is why he wants us to speak in agreement with him and the world. He doesn't want the living Word of God to influence our lives and speech. He wants to keep us re-directed away from the Word of God and its power and dominating force. He wants us to speak words that pervert the truth of God. Satan's battlefield is our mind. Since words carry identity and begin in our thoughts, he wants to be the one to control what we think and speak about, and what we identify with.

The Garden of Eden was God's expression of His perfect will for mankind upon the earth. Then came the serpent. His means of attack was to use words to challenge the thought process by perverting what God had spoken. Adam and Eve chose to listen and think upon Satan's words rather than God's. They came into agreement with Satan's words. In doing so, they turned their backs on God, His words, His system, and His design. By leaning into what Satan was speaking, they broke God's one command not to eat of a specific tree.

"And the LORD God commanded the man, "You are free to eat from any tree in the garden; but you must not eat from the tree of

the knowledge of good and evil, for when you eat from it you will certainly die." Genesis 2:16-17 NIV.

Just as Adam and Eve tuned their ears to Satan's words and turned their backs on God, we do the same, tuning our ears to the frequency of the world.

Satan knows he can weaken our faith with wrong thinking and speaking words that are not established on God's truth. That's why God wants us to turn our attention toward Him and speak life-producing words.

"The life that pleases Me is a life lived in the gratitude of grace, always choosing to walk (conversations, behavior) *with Me in what is right. This is the sacrifice I desire from you. If you do this, more of My salvation will unfold for you."* Psalms 50:23 TPT.

Path of Life

Words are a connecting force in our lives. They come from either a fear-based pattern of thought, expressed in worry, shame, or doubt, or a faith-based pattern of thought, founded in love, hope, encouragement, life, and the truth of God.

One way to think of it is to imagine life and its experiences as a line. Let's call this line the 'Path of Life'. In each direction are two opposing ways of thinking and living, with different sets of consequences. One direction causes you to move forward and experience amazing things that enhance life, while the other produces lost hope, discouragement, and stagnation. The following two columns show examples of what each direction produces:

Life	Death
Health	Sickness
Forgiveness	Unforgiveness
Joy	Bitterness
Gratitude	Complaining
Happiness	Grief
Prosperity	Poverty
Success	Failure
Wisdom	Foolishness
Righteousness	Sin
Love	Hate
Excellence	Mediocrity
Faith	Fear

Every day by choice we live our lives facing and moving in one direction or the other. Whichever we choose to face, means we have our backs toward the opposing direction. The direction we choose affects us in every area of life.

"Set your gaze on the path before you. With fixed purpose, looking straight ahead. Watch where you're going! Stick to the path of truth, and the road will be safe and smooth before you." Proverbs 4:25-26 TPT.

Everything God does is centered on pulling us in one direction only, into life-producing activity. It's never death-producing. Death-producing is like a parasite. It will eat and destroy you from the inside out. We keep it alive by feeding it death-producing words, incorrect actions, and the emotions attached to them.

In the development of your faith, assess everything with this one question: *Is it life-giving or death-producing?* Apply this question to relationships, business and financial decisions, what you think about, where you go, what you eat, the entertainment you choose, and to what your say and how you say it.

"I have set before you life and death, blessing and cursing: therefore choose life, that both thou and thy seed may live." Deuteronomy 30:19 KJV.

Proverbs 18:21 confirms the importance of what we think about and say. *"Death and life are in the power of the tongue"* KJV.

Words are therefore spiritual indicators and carriers of what we believe and in what we place our faith.

After making the above list, I began a determined effort to listen to myself to discover what end of the path I was speaking from, which would reveal the direction I was facing. I found that far too often I faced the wrong way. I had formed habitual thought patterns that were often negative, which turned into words and actions that connected me to lost hope and discouragement. Just because we are Christians doesn't necessarily mean we are always operating, thinking, or speaking in agreement with God's design and His plan for our lives.

One of the most important things to remember is that you will act in a way that is consistent with your thinking. What you focus and meditate on, and every word you say, becomes a blueprint that your mind and body move toward. It will do whatever it can to oblige it.

Where Two or More Agree

There is a principle found in Matthew 18:19, that where two or more witnesses agree, a thing is established. If, on one end of the Path of Life, we have God as a witness, and on the other end we have Satan as a witness, you and I become the deciding witness. If we think, speak, and move in agreement with either one, we come into agreement with them. Do we complain and murmur how bad things are in our lives, give way to negativity, or judge others? Do we gossip, envy, or refuse to forgive? Are we responding instead from a foundation of gratefulness, love and faith, speaking and acting in agreement with hope, truth, and the promises of God's Word? You can clearly see that what you think about and what you say are often strong indicators of the level of your faith.

I challenge you to begin listening to yourself and what comes out of your mouth in conversations. Be as objective as you can, because what you speak is what has been developed in your heart and mind. Remember, *"Whatever comes out of the mouth comes from the heart."* Matthew 15:18 AMP.

"Out of the abundance of the heart the mouth speaketh." Matthew 12:34 KJV.

"For the overflow of what has been stored in your heart will be seen by your fruit and will be heard in your words." Luke 6:45 TPT.

When God brought the Israelites out of Egypt, it was His intention to take them into the Promised Land. However, *"And the people spoke against God and against Moses, Why have you brought us out of Egypt to die in the wilderness?"* Numbers 21:5 AMP.

They were focusing and moving in the wrong direction on their path of life, refusing to place their faith and trust in God. They spoke what was in their hearts - words of unbelief. Though the Promised Land was God's intention, they got what they spoke and perished in the desert. They failed to choose life.

God hasn't changed. Today He is saying, turn your attention and words toward Me. Give thanks and speak in agreement with life and My Word because, *"Whoso offereth praise glorifieth me: and to him that ordereth his conversation aright* (one's thoughts and words, one's life) *will I shew the salvation of God."* Psalms 50:23 KJV.

Destiny of Your Words

If you believe you're facing in the wrong direction on your Path of Life, how do you turn around so you can walk into the destiny God intended? The process is simple, and the words you speak play a major role:

- Thoughts become our words,
- Words turn into action,
- Actions turn into habits,
- Habits become our character,
- Character determines our destiny.

Righteousness is conforming to God's divine will in thought, words, action, habits, and character. Because of that, we are to take *"every thought and purpose captive to the obedience of Christ."* 2 Corinthians 10:5 AMP. We consciously align our words with Christ-like thoughts to keep the process headed in the right direction. Your thoughts and words set your course.

James 3:2-3 tells us, *"We all fail in many areas, but especially with our words. Yet if we're able to bridle the words we say we are powerful enough to control ourselves in every way, and that means our character is mature and fully developed. The tongue is a small part of the body yet it carries great power!* James 3:2, 5 TPT.

If our thinking is not renewed to the Word of God, and we allow the tongue to react uncontrolled, it can spew out words that we may later regret.

The tongue *"is a fickle, unrestrained evil that spews out words full of toxic poison! We use our tongue to praise God and then turn around and curse a person who was made in His very image! Out of the same mouth we pour out words of praise one minute and curses the next ... this should never be!"* James 3: 8-10 TPT.

Words can set the course of your character, what you experience in life, and how people respond to you.

First Words Policy

In making a conscious effort to only speak in agreement with God, His Word, and those things that produce life, I have found that in conversations, or when a situation of stress or crisis arises, or when the devil tries to put the squeeze on, the first words I speak are the most important. They either reflect the faith by which I choose to live, or the doubt which I carry.

I had to learn to take control in those moments. To do that I had to change my thoughts and speak out truth and what I wanted, regardless of how strongly the emotions were pulling me in the wrong direction.

When Jesus reached the end of His 40 day fast, His body was greatly in need of nourishment. At this point the devil came to entice and challenge Him. The devil wanted Him to speak words of defeat, based on His emotions and physical needs. Faith is choosing to listen to the voice of God over the voice of the enemy, or any self-defeating thoughts. Jesus didn't spend time with the devil's words, but rather focused His attention on faith in His Father, and spoke the Word of God to each challenge, 'It is written'... and Satan departed.

If someone cuts you off in traffic, receives the promotion you wanted, or a dark cloud of depression or anxiety comes, how will you respond?

The first words you speak at that crucial point will determine what happens next. It becomes the dividing line in the sand, a self-fulfilling prophecy. Those who deal with the pressure of the moment and speak words of life, move into greater maturity.

Regardless of whether we have been responsible or not in the words we've spoken, we can repent. Repent for the careless words, then make an about face on the Path of Life, knowing you are loved by God. He is full of grace. He has your best interests at heart and desires for you to walk in faith and victory.

I shared earlier that I lived much of my life rooted in emotions that came from disempowering, inner self-beliefs. Though it served no purpose to keep re-living those emotions, that never-ending cycle caused me to remain in a place of stagnation. To live like that, caused me to miss out on life, and stopped all forward motion. Without even knowing it, I attached certain emotions to what I spoke. These easily affected and altered my daily life.

Choosing godly thoughts, exercising faith, and speaking the solution rather than wallowing in the problem, pointed me in the right direction on my path of life. I discovered that if I chose to be strong today, it was most likely I would be strong tomorrow, and the next and the next. My words set in motion new behavioral patterns that God honored.

The tongue is incredible gift we have for making a difference in the world. We have an opportunity to agree with God and speak life into the lives of others. As we enrich another person, we are also enriching ourselves.

Today, practice the art of speaking. Your tomorrows are waiting to hear what you say! So, give voice to your faith, and let what you speak be an expression of your trust in God.

"My inmost being will rejoice when your lips speak what is right." Proverbs 23:16 NIV.

9 / Speak What You Desire

I want to continue a bit further on the importance of consciously speaking what we desire. This is important because our brain will actually pause and listen to what we are speaking. To prove this, do the following simple exercise. Count to twenty in your mind. As you proceed with the counting, have another person ask you to say your name out loud while you are counting silently. Did you notice that the reciting of the numbers in your mind came to a halt the moment you spoke your name out loud? The mind and body stop and pays close attention to what the mouth speaks.

Our body, as well as our faith, pays close attention to what comes out of our mouths. They are both either strengthened or weakened by what we say.

Self-Talk

A problem many of us have is that we get stuck in unhealthy thinking patterns. These thought patterns are what we've become accustomed to and habitually bring forth, without giving them any thought. In fact, reports state that up to 95% of what we do is through unconscious, habitual thoughts. But the question arises, are our thoughts and behavior, and the emotions attached to them, building our faith?

We increase the power of our thoughts when we speak them. If we say something enough, we will believe it. This should cause us to take a closer look at every word that proceeds from our mouths. These include all the clichés and phrases we've been conditioned to speak. We may think of these as insignificant, yet they often launch us further down the same path.

Here is a list of faithless phrases we often speak over ourselves:

- *"I can't lose those last 10 pounds"*
- *"I'm scared to death"*
- *"This commute is killing me"*
- *"I'm dying under the pressure"*
- *"My boss is stressing me out"*
- *"I can't remember"*
- *"I can't stop myself"*
- *"I'm losing my mind"*
- *"I can't do anything right"*
- *"I'm not talented"*
- *"I'm falling apart"*
- *"I'm overwhelmed"*
- *"I'm fat"*
- *"I hate my body"*
- *"I'm starved to death"*
- *"I can never make enough money"*
- *"I'm worn out", "I'm depressed", "I'm tired", "I'm old".*

We rarely say simply, *"I'm thrilled"*, but we do declare, *"I'm thrilled to death."*

You might be thinking, *yeah, but I don't mean those things when I say them.* The Word doesn't talk about the power of what you mean. It says that life and death is in the power of the tongue. Words are containers. They hold expressions of love and faith, or bitterness, worry, and doubt.

With many of these phrases we are constantly telling ourselves something good or something harmful. Even Henry Ford was quoted as saying, *"Whether you think you can, or you think you can't – you're right."* Instead, choose to think and speak what you truly desire to experience and say it in positive way. It's that simple.

And consider the fact of who lives in you. Do you think Jesus would say, or want you saying, *"I AM scared to death"*, *"I AM losing my mind"*, or *"I AM not good enough?"* That's not the I AM that lives within you.

A Powerful Word of Possession

The word 'have' is a powerful word of possession. We speak 'I have' phrases, or others, such as, *"I can't ..."*, or *"Nothing ever ..."*?

When we speak things like this, we are speaking identities into our mind, and when said enough, they drop into our heart. We are revealing what we unconsciously believe to be true, and in what we place our faith.

Paying attention to this is important because of what we say, we tend to take ownership.

It's too easy to tolerate things rather than fight to obtain the promises of God. If we are to walk in faith, we have to change our language, and get rid of negative and judgmental talk. It's time to break these seemingly innocent, unconscious phrases and speak what is life-producing. And move toward what improves our lives and away from what does not. Next time you express a thought incorrectly, stop and re-phrase with a positive slant. Here's an example: *By implementing this new software our goal is to have no more than a 5% error rate.* OR we could state: *By implementing this new software we will achieve a 95% success rate.* By stating the positive we set our mind in the direction of success and achievement.

Another example is instead of stating, *"I'm overwhelmed,"* we would be much better off saying, *"I can handle this"*, *"I can do all things through Christ who strengthens me"*, or *"I'm busy because I'm blessed with opportunities."*

By avoiding negative words and small thinking, we can speak positive, life and faith-producing words, and support big thinking:

- *"God is my strength"*
- *"I'm blessed and favored by God"*
- *"I'm highly motivated"*
- *"I'm proactive"*
- *"I have great coping skills"*

- *"I'm proud of the good job I did"*
- *"I refuse to give in to fear"*
- *"I choose life and live by faith"*
- *"I have a sound mind"*
- *"God is for me and loves me"*
- *"I'm getting in the best shape of my life"*
- *"I appreciate all that I have"*
- *"I'm an amazing person"*
- *"I'm good enough"*
- *"I'm making healthy choices and getting stronger every day"*

7 Day Exercise

Here is a simple, yet revealing exercise that will provide a whole different perspective to the words you choose to speak in daily conversations. Approach everything you speak in the next seven days as if they will *immediately* come to pass. Keep a list because you may be surprised.

Guard Your Words

The Word tells us to: *"Guard your words and you'll guard your life."* Proverbs 13:3 TPT. *"A wholesome tongue is a tree of life."* Proverbs 15:4 KJV. *"The words of the wise soothe and heal."* Proverbs 12:18 TPT.

Our goal is to act and speak as Jesus, so our faith faces the right direction on the Path of Life. What does faith require? It requires that we think before we speak, and that we inquire of the Lord so that we make quality decisions. Remember, quality decisions are the ones you base your life on which allow God to show Himself. Jesus didn't go around speaking foolishly, spouting out self-defeating words, or calling things out that He didn't want. Neither should you. To speak negatively about yourself is not what God's Word says about you or what He thinks about you. It's the opposite. The more conscious you are of your words and identity in Christ, your self-talk improves.

How to Radically Change the Words You Speak

Developing a fully persuaded faith involves a change in your thought life and how you express it; what you say to yourself and others. It can only happen with a renewed mind. To truly renew a mind to the things of God, you must get immersed in the Word.

I remember one particular summer as a young child, being enrolled for swimming lessons by my mother. I stood at the deep end, being told to jump in. I can still feel the reluctance as I looked down at the bottom of the deep end of the pool. But I couldn't learn to swim without being fully immersed. Reluctantly, I did jump in, became fully immersed in the water, and later progressed to swimming across the pool and jumping off the high dive.

Joshua 1: 8 shows us what being immersed in the Word looks like:

"Keep this Book of the Law always on your lips; meditate on it day and night, so that you may be careful to do everything written in it. Then you will be prosperous and successful." NIV.

We often read this verse, remembering the parts about meditating on the Word or doing the commandments of God. But the first thing it says to do is to *let not the Word depart from thy mouth*. That means we speak the Word, not the world. And how long does it say to pray and meditate on the Word and the things of God? Day and night. So, we need to ask ourselves, where is our thought life? And is God at the center of it?

Psalms 1:1-3: *"Blessed is the one whose delight is in the law of the LORD, AND who meditates on his law day and night. That person is like a tree planted by streams of water, which yields its fruit in season and whose leaf does not wither - whatever they do prospers."* NIV.

In another verse we are told to *"Pray without ceasing"*, and *"In every thing give thanks: for this is the will of God in Christ Jesus concerning you."* I Thessalonians 5:17-18 KJV.

To radically re-new your mind means to turn away from anything that distracts you from Him. It means you separate yourself from the world as much as possible and every day spend more time with God. Some of the areas that may need to get re-prioritized are spending too much time focused on the news, TV, radio, newspaper, worldly entertainment, and hours surfing the net.

That doesn't mean you stop living your life, doing your job, taking care of responsibilities, or having down time to relax. But it does mean you devote more time to what is most important.

Here are a few tips:

- Begin each day with reading the Word. Allow God to wash you in the Word, and reveal Himself more deeply by meditating on what you've read.

- Speak His Word over your day, and any personal declarations based on His promises (personal self-talk).

- Find a church that actively teaches faith, and has the same desire and passion for God as you.

- While driving in your car, if it's possible, listen to recorded faith-filled messages, or audible inspiring, faith-building books.

- Begin watching free online Christ-centered programing, and archived services. Read more faith-building, inspiring books.

- Spend time with like-minded people, who love the Lord.

When you consider the fact that the average person watches 4 hours of television every day, and combined with surfing the net and Facebook, that equates to about 13 years of one's life. It's not that watching TV or being on the computer is wrong. It's whether or not the Word of God takes first billing in your heart over these other things.

The exciting thing about growing in the Lord, is that it will change the way you think. It will change what you hold dear and drop these things down into the heart of you. Which of course, changes how you talk.

If you are like me, the more your mind is re-newed, the less patience you will have for all the foolishness and babble of the world. It will make you more protective of your spirit and mind. You will think differently, speak differently, and God's faith in your life will begin to soar.

His Word is *"Life unto those who find it."* Proverbs 4:22 KJV.

"Stop imitating the ideals and opinions of the culture around you,
but be inwardly transformed by the Holy Spirit through
a total reformation of how you think.
This will empower you to discern God's will as you live
a beautiful life, satisfying and perfect in his eyes."
Romans 12:2 TPT.

10 / Word of God

We ended the last chapter by discussing renewing the mind into order to change our words. But since a major part of developing a faith that is fully persuaded involves the renewing, or transforming of our mind, and the fact that this is an ever-ongoing process, we need to dive a bit deeper.

To transform your mind, you do this using the Word of God. In Christian terms, we yield to the Holy Spirit, and allow Him to mold us into the image of Christ. Which means, we feed upon the Word of God and allow the Holy Spirit to take it and give us new understandings, new desires, and ultimately a new transformed life.

But you have an adversary, that old flesh devil. He is a liar and a thief and will do anything to snatch the Word, minimize its effects, and keep you tangled up with your old self, its desires, and the world around you.

Satan is very aware that when you accepted Christ your spirit was regenerated. You are spiritually a new creation.

"Therefore, if anyone is in Christ, he is a new creation; old things have passed away; behold, all things have become new." 2 Corinthians 5:17 NKJV.

The old thing that passed away was your sin nature. The sin nature you've had since birth is gone, due to your new rebirth in Christ. Your spirit is now one with Him. But your soul (mind, will, and emotions) on the other hand, still has to be renewed, which is a life-long process. So, how do you do that?

You first used the blood of Christ to remove your sin and the bondage to it. Now, you use the blood and the Word of God to get sin off of you, off and out of your flesh. It's been in you and on you for so long, it often gets embedded into your mind and acts out in the body. Your next step is a process of spiritual maturity, allowing the truth of God to become your daily reality. Which is why the Word instructs us to renew the mind, so that you align yourself with the Word of God, and the voice of God which now occupies your spirit.

Let me give you an example:

I remember one particular day being attacked in my thoughts, and I knew every button was being pushed to intensify it. Depression, lack of self-worth, and condemnation hit me like a tsunami. As I sat there in this emotional darkness, I heard the Lord's voice within me say, *"Satan wants to be the author and finisher of your faith."* That was all it took! I rose up and said, "Jesus is the Author and Finisher of my faith, and because I'm in Him, I will not be robbed of the riches of His glory."

The attack that day came from inner beliefs developed in childhood. These beliefs turn into incorrect stories, attached with emotions that I told myself over and over. They were so ingrained in me, they became habitual thought patterns of identity that kept me stuck. The enemy was always there to spur them on, and used them to keep me in emotional poverty most of my life.

The battleground of the mind is where he will always attack. And as basic or simple as it may be, I was never taught how to defeat him; never taught that in the emotional darkness of the moment I could defeat him by standing in faith using the Word of God. I had to stumble across this and learn it for myself. I share this to emphasize why feeding your spirit with the Word and allowing it to transform the mind is so vital.

Though you are a child of the King, Satan doesn't want your identity in Christ to take root. He wants you to live as a commoner, worried, stressed, sick, discouraged, and defeated. He doesn't want you to fix your eyes on the unseen things God has in mind for you. And he certainly doesn't want you to live in faith and take possession of what Christ has already made available to you. All these things are really just strongholds that need to be torn down, and rebuilt with God's truth.

God's Design

To better understand the playing field, so you can begin renewing your mind, let's first take a closer look at what's really taking place within your mind and your physical brain.

The brain and mind are not the same thing. The brain is an amazing, highly developed piece of software with tons of circuitry. In fact, science has discovered that the brain has the capability to store a minimum of 3 million years worth of information.

The mind, on the other hand, works through the physical organ of the brain. We think with our mind, but store the thoughts in our brain. The brain will cease and decay upon physical death, but awareness of who we are will remain, because our mind is part of the soul.

The mind is the core of our mental makeup. The spirit and the mind (soul) are both components of the inward, spiritual part of us. Together they form the heart of who we are.

Reports tell us we have around 50,000 – 60,000 thoughts per day. Some report as much as 70,000. And according to research, as many as 98 percent of them are exactly the same we had the day before!

But even more significant, reports tell us that for a large percentage of people, up to 80% of our thoughts are negative. This is toxic thinking. Toxic is defined as, *dangerous, injurious, harmful, destructive, unsafe, and lethal.*

Healthy and Toxic Thoughts

Obviously, thoughts can either be healthy or toxic. When we operate and respond in love, aligning our thoughts with the richness of the truth of God's Word, we produce healthy thinking in our mind. Toxic thinking produces anxiety, bitterness, unforgiveness, depression, and fear. If as much as 80 percent of thoughts are negative or toxic, just imagine the damage these do to the brain cells and the body. They actually become roadblocks to our physical health, as well as our faith.

When a new thought arrives in our conscious mind a structure in the brain is formed to hold that thought. The thought is only temporarily held unless we give it more attention. The thought will last 24-48 hours. If it is not reinforced by further thought, further study, or spoken, the structure formed to hold that thought will denature and the thought will dissipate. However, the more we hear something, and think and talk about it, the more it's re-enforced by physical structures in the brain formed to hold those thoughts. Simply stated, we've then built a home to hold that thought so we can re-visit it over and over. The longer the thought becomes part of our thinking process, it will be moved from the conscious to the unconscious, and create automatic, habitual response patterns of belief, behavior, thoughts, and emotions. Why emotions? Because any emotion attached to the information also becomes part of the long-term memory. The more emotional an experience, good or bad, the deeper it gets embedded into the unconscious. What you believe to be true will be binding upon you.

"Above all else, guard your heart, for everything you do flows from it" Proverbs 4:23 NIV.

Strong negative beliefs and their accompanying emotions sent me down a dark hole for decades. Worry and fear caused me to make poor decisions and hurt others, though that was never my intent. Toxic emotions and fear will cause you to be someone you don't like, and keep you from hearing the Spirit of God who wants to direct your life.

And consider this fact, if the thoughts we have today are basically the same we had yesterday, how can we ever expect true change to take place with the same thought patterns. The truth is, we can't. For change to take place we must change our thinking and act upon it.

One of the keys to breaking harmful cycles of habitual negative thought and behavior patterns, is to know that when these arise, you have just seconds to decide what to do with it. In these few moments you can either feed it or starve it. This is what I learned to do in my own life. When the defeating thoughts began to flood my mind and extreme emotional darkness pushed hard, I had to find the strength to speak out loud the Word of God declaring who I was in Christ. I noticed that when I did this throughout the day the emotions weakened and the defeating thoughts showed up less and less. What a personal breakthrough that was!

To do this, and for faith to grow and become an immovable force in your life, anything that attempts to alter what the Word of God says about you or others must be dealt with quickly! First acknowledge it for what it is and its accompanying emotions, then minimize it by taking authority over it and casting it down. Casting down means you immediately do not tolerate it in any fashion.

Change your thoughts, begin thanking God, change your physical stance, and speak the truth of God's Word. In other words, move your body, move your mouth, and mind, choosing resurrection life over the death-producing negative thoughts, emotions, and actions.

"Cast down imaginations, and every high thing that exalteth itself against the knowledge of God, and bringing into captivity every thought to the obedience of Christ." 2 Corinthians 10:5 KJV.

When we take authority and minimize a thought, we weaken the structure that houses that thought. Physical substances in the brain can actually change, as we build new, transforming patterns of thought in the mind. You will notice old thoughts become fewer and fewer. The more Word of God you have in you, the better your mind is able to filter out the unwanted, disempowering thoughts. The longer those thoughts become part of your thinking process, they get moved from the conscious to the unconscious, and create automatic, habitual response patterns of belief, behavior, thoughts, and emotions. Do this, and the devil sees that he can no longer push your around.

Developing New Habits

I grew up being told that it takes 21 days to develop a new habit. That is partially correct. New habits can begin to be established in that time. But just like dieting, 21 days of dieting won't produce a lifetime of weight loss. However, a change in thinking will. It always comes back to our underlying thinking patterns.

Getting rid of old, toxic thinking patterns and developing healthy embedded new ones, actually take approximately 30-65 days. One to two months is relatively a short period of time, but due to the fact that we live in a society of instant gratification, and where New Year's resolutions fail within 4-5 days, sticking with it takes a committed, resolved effort.

In 21 days, you can tear down old thought structures and build new ones. Once you do this, and continue to think and speak new thoughts for another 40 days or more, it will become a habitual thought and belief, without consciously having to think about it. It becomes a part of who you are as you renew your mind! Allow the Word of God to become who you are!

And don't quit after the 60 days or so. You continue in the Word, allowing it to fill you for the rest of your life because living by faith, fully persuaded in your thought life is a life long career from which you never retire!

Know, that even if you've spent years creating a chaotic mind and a dysfunctional, toxic brain, the mind and the physical brain respond quickly when you make a decision to reach out to God and begin to focus your attention on His Word.

It's not something that your doctor can do for you, nor your best friend. You have to do the work, and as we discussed above, it takes time. It begins by seeing yourself as God created you, not what you've become. You are made in His image and likeness, and designed and wired for love. You have been given a sound mind, and when you accepted Christ, you became His new creature and now have God's spiritual DNA running through you.

Every day set aside time to focus on the rebuilding process of your thought life. Think of speaking, reading, and meditating on the Word of God as exercising new muscles. The more you do it, the bigger and stronger those muscles become. Think of developing faith as developing a strong spiritual grip. It's time for you to become a muscular spiritual giant! So, whatever that old story is for you, it needs to be replaced. It's more than just positive thinking. It's choosing to be a faith warrior and taking hold of what Christ died to give you.

A great exercise is to write out your new story. The story of what God says about you. The story of what you want your life to look like. The story of who you really are and now choose to be. Make it compelling with emotions attached to it. The more personal and emotional, the greater impact it will have upon you. Then read it every day, speak it out loud, and develop new habits that support it. Allow it to define who you really are in Christ.

Let me share, as an example a portion of my personal declaration I speak over my life. I speak it in third person, out loud, and with emotion. Speaking in third person has shown to build you up, like a supportive friend would do. Also, it can cause you to gravitate toward more positive messages about yourself.

"David, you wake up younger, wiser, healthier and stronger in the Lord every day. You've got the Word of God! The spoken Word, the written Word, and the Living Word Himself, the Anointed One Jesus Christ. Yes, the Word is life, energy, and vitality to you, and the Word is health and healing to every cell in your body!

And David, you've been given a sound mind, with focus, clarity, and understanding, recall and memory, directed by the Holy Spirit, yes David, that's who you are and what you have all the days of your life!

And why, because you've not been given some things, but rather according to His divine power, He's given you ALL things according to LIFE, and godliness ... and exceedingly great and precious promises! And they all find their fullness in Him – David, by His stripes you are healed, you've been made the righteousness of God, you are an heir of God and joint heir with Jesus Christ! You've been taken out of the spirit of darkness and into the spirit of light. You've been redeemed. Yes David, that's why you wake up younger, wiser, and healthier, and stronger in the Lord every day. You are in a blood covenant relationship with the Lord God Almighty! YES, YES, YES!"

Search the scriptures for verses connected to your identity in Christ and integrate them into a personal declaration.

Remember, victory is your inherited right of being *in Christ*. When the enemy of your soul turns up the volume of his voice, tune your ear to the voice of God's Word. That's exactly what Jesus did when being tempted for 40 days in the wilderness, and the enemy departed. In Christ, you can act and think from a position of victory.

We get to decide what we fill our brain with, what our mind focuses on, and how much our spirit is fed. When we secure the Word of God within us, it becomes *"implanted within our nature, for the Word of Life has power to continually deliver us."* James 1:21 TPT.

11 / With Him

There is a huge difference in simply knowing about Christ and truly knowing Him. Knowing Him comes from a place of relationship or abiding with Him.

What does abiding look like? The Greek word for *abide* is *meno*. It means to stay in one place, to remain, to continue or permanently abide. It's a lasting relationship. A place of intimacy with Him and the power of His resurrection. It's in this type of relationship where you develop your identity and fully persuaded faith.

You do this by making the Word of God a high priority in your life. You schedule alone time with Him and His Word, meditating on it, and talking and communicating with Him. He wants you to share your thoughts with Him, and He wants to share His with you. He wants you to ask questions and He desires to impart spiritual knowledge and direction to you. He doesn't want you to simply believe *in* Him. He wants you to *believe* Him because that's the way faith works.

This is what the Creator of the Universe desires of you and me. And out of such a love and trust relationship, comes more than we could ever imagine.

"For it is not from man that we draw our life but from God as we are being joined to Jesus, the Anointed One. And now he is our God-given wisdom, our virtue, our holiness, and our redemption." 1 Corinthians 1:30 TPT.

With Him, you are an heir of God and joint heir with Christ: *"For the Holy Spirit makes God's fatherhood real to us as he whispers into our innermost being, You are God's beloved child! And since we are his true children, we qualify to share all his treasures, for indeed, we are heirs of God himself. And since we are joined to Christ, we also inherit all that he is and all that he has."* Romans 8:16-17 TPT. Being joined together with Christ means we also inherit suffering because we bear His name, but far greater, we share in His glory.

In Revelation 1:8, it states *"I am the Alpha and the Omega— the beginning and the end," says the Lord God. "I am the one who is, who always was, and who is still to come—the Almighty One."* NLT.

He is the great I AM, and the author and finisher of your faith. He's at your beginning and He is your end. In Him is the spirit of life, wholeness, and all things pertaining to life. And because the great I AM is in you, you can speak I AM words … I am more than enough. I am healed. I am the righteousness of God. I am a new creature and all things are new. I am blessed and highly favored because I am loved unconditionally by Him. In Him, I am being perfected in His love, so that I can love others.

All that He is ... so are you! *"All that Jesus now is, so are we in this world."* 1 John 4:17 TPT.

But it's knowing that everything you have is based on His efforts, not yours. He paid for it at Calvary. He is your source and security. Everything you received at salvation is in Christ. In other words, you have your life in Christ Jesus. *"For in him we live."* Acts 17:28 KJV.

It is the privilege of abiding with the Lord, in full trust that He is able to perform every word He has ever spoken, every promise ever given, and through the blood of Christ, meet every need ever expressed.

For it was always in his perfect plan to adopt us as his delightful children, through our union with Jesus, the Anointed One, so that his tremendous love that cascades over us would glorify his grace - for the same love he has for Jesus, he has for us. And this unfolding plan brings him great pleasure!

Since we are now joined to Christ, we have been given the treasures of redemption by his blood - the total cancellation of our sins all because of the cascading riches of his grace" (Ephesians 1:5-7 TPT).

"Therefore God exalted him to the highest and gave him the name that is above every name, that at the name of Jesus every knee should bow, in heaven and on earth and under the earth." Philippians 2:9-10 NIV.

Being in relationship with Him, knowing the love He has for you, and that He has elevated you in every way, should leave absolutely no doubt that you can believe and stand in fully persuaded faith in Him and on His Word.

It was God's design, His decision, that we live abundantly. He intends for us to live faith-filled lives, as overcomers. Overcoming is a continuous action of faith exercised in Him and with Him. We overcome the world and its systems because Jesus overcame it all!

Final Thoughts

"Not one promise from God is empty of power, for nothing is impossible with God!" Luke 1:37 TPT. The verse doesn't say that through *knowing about* God nothing is impossible. It says, *with* God nothing is impossible. As we stated, 'with' refers to being in relationship *with Him*, a place of not just believing in Him, but believing Him!

It may seem un-imaginable, but God wants to be wanted by you! He wants to lavish you with a life beyond measure, reward you, and direct your life through a close-knit, covenant relationship. In knowing Him through relationship, which passes all intellectual

94

knowledge, we move past the wisdom of this world into revelation of intimacy with Him!

"That your faith should not stand in the wisdom of men, but in the power of God." 1 Corinthians 2:5 KJV.

God wants to bless you more than you could ever imagine.

"For we come to God in faith knowing that he is real and that he rewards the faith of those who give all their passion and strength into seeking him." Hebrews 11:6 TPT.

When the Word becomes alive in your spirit, embedded into your mind, will, and emotions, it becomes who you are. Then when you ask in faith, in agreement with Him, and in the power of His name, you know you have it because there is no doubt in the integrity and power of God's Word and His ability to perform it. That is fully persuaded faith!

"If ye abide (remain) *in me,* **and my words abide** (remain) **in you,** *ye shall ask what ye will, and it shall be done unto you."* John 15:7 KJV.

So, we continually put the Word in our eyes, ears, and mouth. Speak it out and act upon it in faith, as we forgive others and daily recognize how loved we are by Him. Our job is to believe His Word, speak it, and hold fast to our confession of faith (Hebrews 10:23 AMP), continually giving Him the glory in all things because it is not us, but He that has done the work. He will continue to perfect us.

"That God would grant you, according to the riches of His glory, to be strengthened with ability by His spirit in your inner self,

so that Christ may dwell in your heart by faith, that you, being rooted and grounded in love, could comprehend and know the love of Christ that you might be filled with all the fullness of God. The One who is able to do exceedingly abundantly above all we ask or think, according to the power and love that works within us." Ephesians 3:17-19 KJV paraphrased by author).

The world is quick to see any inconsistencies. When trials come, and they will, its how we handle those that the world remembers. Even when old emotions attached to past hurts, or feelings of not being good enough arise, having the Word of God in us, allows us to stand our ground and fight through the trials from a place of victory, not defeat.

Everything we need is in Christ, who is in you to meet every need of every circumstance, any trial that presents itself.

"According as his divine power hath given unto us all things that pertain unto life and godliness, through the knowledge of him that hath called us to glory and virtue: Whereby are given unto us exceeding great and precious promises: that by these ye might be partakers of the divine nature, having escaped the corruption that is in the world through lust." 2 Peter 1:3-4 KJV.

As you journey daily along your Path of Life, choose life by always moving in the direction of His life-giving promises. Moving forward in faith maintains the victory Christ died to obtain. All wisdom, joy, love, peace, redemption, deliverance, health, and finances, the completed finished work of the cross is yours.

I trust the material in this book has provided new perspectives, new revelations, and some new responsibilities.

I hope it has helped you better define your relationship with God, His Word, and that you will pursue living a life founded on uncompromised, fully persuaded faith.

Though God has provided many things for our well-being in the physical or natural realm, His Word is above it all. The power of His Word created you, and it will continue to sustain you.

*"For I know the plans I have for you," declares the L*ORD*,*

"plans to prosper you and not to harm you,

plans to give you hope and a future, therefore choose life,"

and "let the faith of God be in you!"

Jeremiah 29:11 NIV / Deuteronomy 30:19 AMP / Mark 11:22 TPT

* * * * * * *

PS ... I have included an Appendix at the end of the book to address the subject of health and how the state of one's health can war against faith. The subject is seldom addressed, yet one that greatly affects the body of Christ.

Prayer for Salvation

A person's first step in developing a fully persuaded faith, is receiving Jesus Christ as Lord.

If you happen to read this book and are not a Christian, I invite you to accept Jesus as your Lord and Savior. If you mean it in your heart and call upon His name, you will be saved.

Prayer: *Jesus, I repent of my sins and receive your gift of forgiveness and the fullness of Your salvation. I renounce Satan and any ties he has to my life, and proclaim that Jesus is the Son of God, who came to earth, was crucified, resurrected, and now lives. Please take my life Lord and use it for your glory. Amen*

———————————

"By constantly using your faith, the life of Christ will be released deep inside you, and the resting place of his love will become the very source and root of your life."

Ephesians 3:17 TPT

Appendix: Health that Wars Against Faith

I believe that we have a covenant right for divine healing and health. But I'm not going to focus so much on that aspect, but rather discuss what's seldom talked about in churches - natural health and the influence it can have on one's faith. Sickness, disease, and cognitive decline are epidemic worldwide, and for the Christian, can war against developing or maintaining one's fully persuaded faith.

The enemy comes to steal, kill, and destroy and will use any means he can to weaken the Word of God and diminish one's faith. Satan will go after the state of your mind and body to attack faith whenever he can. Let's be honest, when dealing with a physical ailment or disease, it's easy to get fearful and discouraged and lose hope. It often turns one's focus inward rather than outward. It can rob us of time, money, and of what we could accomplish. It can weaken the strength of our thought life and trigger unwanted emotions.

Those emotions bring a stress that can feel like a heavy weight. *"Anxiety in the heart of a man weighs it down."* Proverbs 12:25 NAS.

As it bears down on one's thought life, stress, worry and anxiety shuts down the healing processes of the body.

But to stay fit and healthy is a lot like developing faith. It takes action. Faith without action is dead, and desiring to live a healthy life without action is also as good as dead. Action includes standing on God's Word and adopting lifestyle habits that support wellness.

One of the most important things to understand is that there is no way to get healing and long-term health except through the power of God. It can come either directly through His divine healing or through the design God built into the human body to heal itself.

No doctor or drug can heal you. It's God's design of the body that repairs and heals itself. Proper care of the human body that supports healing includes: nutritional building blocks, proper hydration, regular exercise, elimination of foods that create health issues, a daily quiet time with the Lord, and adopting an attitude of gratitude. Did the last two surprise you? As we discussed earlier, renewing the soul is vital, not only for spiritual growth but physical health.

In addition, we must understand how the nervous system plays an enormous part in our health and in the healing process. The nervous system has two sides, the sympathetic and parasympathetic. One is your fight, flight, or freeze state. It's where worry, fear, and anxiety can hang out. The other is your rest, digest, and heal state. The devil knows this well, which is why he wants to create turmoil, worry, and fear in your life. The body struggles to heal when a person is in a continual state of stress.

When God pointed me in a different direction 33 years ago, I walked away from the standard American diet. I had to first admit, I was hurrying my future demise through my dietary choices. With God's help, I kicked the sugar addiction that plagued me and I implemented action by developing new dietary habits.

There is not a day that goes by that I am not continually grateful to the Lord for this intervention, revelation, and transformation in my life.

Two Categories of Food

When I walked away from the standard American diet, one of the first things I learned was how to differentiate between foods. You may hear people saying that one food is good for you, while another is bad. And as we all know, there are varying opinions out there about food. For me, it wasn't about good or bad because that was man's opinion. I discovered that God was all about life. I began viewing foods as to which were life-producing, because either food supports and builds healthy cellular structures or weakens them. If it is the latter, a person ages faster, immune function diminishes, internal imbalances are created, and inflammation increases, which all lead to *unnecessary* and unwanted degenerative diseases.

God designed the physical body with an amazing ability to rejuvenate and heal itself. The body will do whatever it can to keep you alive. It is always seeking balance and repair. **BUT** for it to do so, it takes balancing stress, correct nutrition, detoxification, and maintaining high cellular function.

When we were young, we had the ability to bounce back and repair quite quickly. But far too often, poor nutrition, lack of exercise, compromised intestinal tracts, faulty cellular activity, inflammation, incorrect gene expression, increased oxidative and chronic stress, and years of prescription medication use, all damage and take their toll on the body. All these things change the inner terrain of the body so that it no longer has the ability to repair and heal, or ward off unpleasant aging symptoms as it once did. The key is to choose life.

The Word says in Deuteronomy 30:23, *"I call Heaven and Earth to witness against you today: I place before you Life and Death. Choose life so that you and your children will live"* KJV.

Of course, food was not the center focus of this verse when it was given, but it applies because we are operating under laws and principles established by God. As Christians we can seek to live under spiritual laws, but if we ignore God's natural laws that affect our physical body, it will suffer the consequences. When God placed before us life and death, He also gave us the answer, *choose life!* It applies to every decision placed before us, including our dietary and lifestyle habits. And this is truer today than perhaps any time in history.

Our enemy, Satan, hates us and has been involved in the food industry since creation. Satan's sole aggressive intent toward us is found in John 10:10: *"The thief cometh not, but for to steal, and to kill, and to destroy."* KJV.

When I was a young boy, I remember Devil's food cake being a popular dessert. Today, Satan has moved way past sugary desserts, and influenced almost the entire food industry. The standard American diet should be renamed, the Devil's diet, because it is full of food products that are processed, stripped of nutrition, energy, genetically modified, full of chemicals, preservatives, and other harmful and artificial substances – none of which meet God's design for sustained health. These age us faster and lead to chronic illness. It's a 'steal, kill, and destroy' diet, which also includes a high intake of animal and dairy products, added sugars, white/wheat flour, saturated fats, fried and fast foods, with little intake of organic fruits and vegetables. I think you can see to which end of the Path of Life you will find this type of diet and to what end it leads.

Yes, I understand that we love convenience and the ease of quick prep and fast food. Let's face it, these foods taste pretty darn good, and manufacturers design them so that the more we eat, the more we crave. Our waist size continues to expand, and we develop all types of diseases. This deception within the food industry has unfortunately taken many in the church captive.

James 3:16 tells us, *"For where strife is, there is confusion and every evil work."* KJV. This verse has many spiritual applications, but let me use its principle and apply it to dietary choices.

When we eat the standard American diet, high in the foods mentioned above, and low in fresh organic fruits and vegetables, we are eating food that creates strife or chronic stress in the body. These types of dietary choices, along with emotional stressors, cause great miscommunication throughout the body, including in the brain. We experience hormonal imbalances, damage to DNA, inflammation, blood flow changes, incorrect gene expression, cellular mutation, poor digestion and assimilation of nutrients, and the list goes on.

The Apostle Paul said, *"So here's what I want you to do, God helping you: Take your everyday, ordinary life - your sleeping, eating, going-to-work, and walking-around life - and place it before God as an offering. Embracing what God does for you is the best thing you can do for him. Don't become so well adjusted to your culture that you fit into it without even thinking."* Romans 12:1-2 MSG.

We do ourselves a great disservice by not being educated in the area of personal health, and as a result, we don't look much different from the rest of the world. We have an adversary who knows if He can break down our physical bodies and attack our thoughts, he has a huge tool for weakening the spiritual part of us, and diminishing our ability to live with fully persuaded faith.

You are a child of God, and health and wellness are within your reach. You can turn back the clock, slow aging, and yes, even prevent many degenerative diseases as you get older! It's just a matter of choice.

In continuing to tackle the subject of health, let me share a few observations and leave you with the task of personal assessment.

Observation #1:

America has some of the best medical and emergency facilities in the world, with amazing life-saving procedures, and state-of-the-art equipment, run and operated by highly trained individuals. Praise God for these facilities, emergency services, and doctors who truly desire the best for their patients. But keep in mind, doctors must often conform to government regulations and provide treatment based on what they've been trained to do, which is not in the area of nutrition and natural approaches.

*I think we fail to understand that **the cause of a disease is NOT the result of a drug deficiency**,* yet too often a drug is what is sought or prescribed as the answer. In fact, often it's in what we place our faith.

Doctors and drugs don't cure disease. A calm mind and clean body functioning as it is designed, with a strong immune and repair system, heals itself. In other words, it's working with God's design of the body that prevents and cures disease.

I am thankful for modern medicine, and prescription drugs definitely have their place. But all too often they only suppress symptoms and disrupt normal cellular function. They're designed to provide symptomatic benefit, and they do that by stopping functions of the body. They can be lifesaving when faced with an emergency, or provide needed help and relief for the moment, but we tend to use them as Band-Aids for symptoms, while not taking steps to address the underlying cause.

If I offered you an apple and told you that in eating it there were possible side effects which include, vomiting, nausea, headache, chest pain, diminished liver function, blurred vision, shortness of breath, depression, diarrhea, or possible death, would you eat it? Probably not. But if a doctor prescribes a drug with the same side effects most people don't think twice as they quickly reach for a glass of water to wash the medication down.

We have become a nation of drug addicts, and a large percentage of them are senior citizens. Not a complimentary statement, but one that unfortunately is true. Americans buy more medicine per person than any other country. It is reported that 75% of adults over the age of 65 are taking a prescription medicine for a chronic disease, and many over 65 are taking five or more medicines at one time. Most of them have no understanding of what true health care is. They have no idea that there are products and supplements that address their health concerns, and yes, even help reverse chronic conditions. This saddens me, but this is the reality of our health care system.

Here are three key questions to ask your doctor when being prescribed a drug or treatment, especially when it comes to cancer:

- Will this drug or treatment cure me?
- What are the potential complications and side effects?
- Will this drug or treatment boost immune function, or diminish it?

No matter how we view pharmaceuticals, they are big business and these companies continue to rake in unspeakable amounts of money every day, to the tune of billions of dollars a year.

Whether or not we see eye to eye on this subject, I think we can agree that drug use in this country has crossed over into insanity. It's part of a system that is geared for managing disease, not curing it.

Here's a suggestion: When taking your daily prescription, each time speak out loud and say, *"I have the healing power of God working in me, and there will come a day when I no longer need this medicine."*

Observation #2:

Most people won't initiate change until they reach the point where pain, lack of energy, an unwanted diagnosis, or the desire to lose weight becomes a strong enough motivator. Though a healthy diet and preventative care is the best policy, it's often the last resort. Even when faced with chronic health issues, many still refuse to be helped, opting to put their faith in disease management rather than personal health care.

But as a word of encouragement, you are never too old to start and there is never a condition that you can't improve upon. It's far easier to prevent something than it is to reverse it, but with a determined mindset, dietary and lifestyle habits and specific health supplements, I've seen some amazing turnabouts. Why is this? Because they took specific action steps to improve the inner terrain of their body so it could repair and heal as God designed it.

So the question becomes, will you wait for your current health condition to worsen, or possibly for an unwanted diagnosis before making healthier choices?

Observation #3:

Often people say they eat healthy, yet when I see what fills their grocery carts, the choices they make at restaurants, and listen to how they talk, I see a different side.

The Word refers to our bodies as temples. *"Do you not know that your bodies are temples of the Holy Spirit, who is in you, whom you have received from God? You are not your own; you were bought at a price. Therefore honor God with your bodies."* 1 Corinthians 6:19-20 NIV.

This does not mean that we are to worship our bodies, but rather respect and properly care for them, understanding their Biblical intention and value.

Solomon was given instructions for the specific design of the physical temple that would be God's dwelling place. It was the Lord's temple and considered holy. Solomon and the people honored God by keeping it in proper order.

What does it mean then to honor God with our temple? Though refraining from immorality is one aspect, we also honor Him by being a people of excellence and integrity in all we think, say, and do. Part of that integrity and excellence includes properly caring for our bodies and making the decision that we are no longer going to do anything that harms it. Whereas Solomon respected God's instruction and design of the temple, we all too often dishonor ours by putting into it whatever our taste buds desire without discerning whether or not it does the body good or if we are honoring God's design of it.

In what I call my former life, a life of sugar addiction and eating the standard America diet, my way of eating was slowly destroying my physical temple. Though I was totally oblivious to this, I was not eating as unto the Lord, but unto myself. I was treating my body more like a shack, filling it with mostly garbage.

I find it interesting, that in 2000, at the turn of the century, it was shown that only about 3% of the population lived healthy lifestyles. This included those who didn't smoke, were at their natural weight, ate 5 or more servings of fresh fruits and vegetables daily, and exercised regularly. Fifteen years later, the same study showed that only 1% of the population met these criteria.

If we ignore the principles of health, the body will react accordingly. It's a pretty simple equation.

When I stopped eating the American culture's way, *food became my medicine rather than my poison*. I also came to the realization that true health care takes place at home, in what you think, what you consume, and what you do, day after day. I sought out foods that contain life, were nutrient-dense, supported cellular frequency and function, and built a strong immune system. I found specific products and supplements (formulations) that addressed rejuvenation and healing, and supported health at the cellular level.

As a former sugar addict, I can attest, if you begin eating real food and follow a healthy protocol, your body will adjust and begin to crave what's good. You will actually start to dislike a lot of the other. Taste buds and desires can be changed!

Final Comments

We must ask ourselves: *How will I put my life in order and align it according to God's design spiritually, naturally, personally, and professionally within the culture of today?*

When God pointed me in a different direction, it was my mind that changed first. I was headed in one direction, and He caused me

110

to see its consequences. I developed a new vision for my future. I quickly adopted a whole new thinking pattern as to how I was going to take care of this body. My body and taste buds followed my mindset and welcomed real nutrition. Developing a compelling vision is the first discipline for true change and greater success in any area of life.

We can't simply sit back and wait for God to wave His hand over us to become spiritually strong with fully persuaded faith, without getting into His Word and feeding our spirit and soul. And we can't be a couch-potato, sit all day behind a desk, bask in the dietary culture of today, or rely on prescription drugs, expecting to have amazing health the rest of our lives. We have to become more educated in what true health care really is and not get distracted by all those fad diets. Instead, follow the principles of healthy lifestyle habits.

Health is simple, but it is a choice. A choice we make every day. I encourage you to become more educated in what comprises a healthy diet and lifestyle. Fall in love with the Word of God, meditate on it, and spend time with the Lord. *"That our faith should not stand in the wisdom of men, but in the power of God."* 1 Corinthians 2:5 KJV.

If a health issue arises, seek God's wisdom in the matter. He may tell you to proceed with the medical procedure, use the medication, or change your diet and tackle the health issue through proper nutrition, specific health products, or a combination of things, including standing on His Word. And as stated earlier, if you are taking a prescription, believe that it is only for a season, taking steps to address the underlying cause so you can get off of it for good.

In addition, search your heart. Is there any unforgiveness, bitterness, or judgmental attitudes that could be causing your illness and might be in the way of your healing? Have you been connected to anything with demonic ties? Perhaps there is something generational that needs prayer and repentance in order to be broken.

Whatever you decide to do, make sure you have peace about it, doing it in faith. Also beware, depending upon the issue or diagnosis, the medical community often invokes fear, telling someone they must proceed immediately with their medical protocols and prescriptions. Don't let fear dictate your decisions. Pray about it. Seek the Holy Spirit's leading and peace.

And if making a change in diet is hard for you, cultivate a mindset centered on being healthy and fit for your spouse and children. Better yet, do it for the Lord. And don't try to go it alone. Develop a support team. It will greatly increase your odds for successs.

Remember, whether healing or health comes through prayer and the power of God's Word, or a change in diet and lifestyle, it is still God because it's what He has designed.

There is enough in this world that wars against us on a daily basis. The last thing any of us want is to deal with health issues. I personally have found that being energized, healthy, and fit is a big support to standing strong in my faith. There is an inner strength that accompanies being healthy.

So, as you and I go forward, whether it be dietary or in any area of life, may we make quality, life-producing decisions, walk fully persuaded in God's Word, and accomplish everything the Lord has planned for us.

For more information and resources: imaginewhatcouldbe.com

"When the Son of Man comes,

will he find faith on the earth?"

Luke 18:8 NIV.

Notes: